Dick Wh

A panto

Norman Ro

Samuel French – London
New York – Sydney – Toronto – Hollywood

CHARACTERS

(In order of their appearance)

Fairy Bow-bells
King Rat
Alderman Fitzwarren
Idle Jack
Sarah, the Cook
Dick Whittington
Tommy, the cat
Captain Port
First Mate Starboard
Alice Fitzwarren
Sultana Bunn, Ruler of Morocco
Zubediah, her favourite slave

Chorus of Citizens (with some small speaking roles)
Fairies, Dancing Girls and **Men, Sailors, Slaves,** etc.

Junior Chorus of **Rats, Fairies,** etc.

Babes as required

SYNOPSIS OF SCENES

ACT I

ACT II

For

Alan and Irene Wright

in recognition of their fortitude in surviving
the "friendship" of the Robbins family

A licence issued by Samuel French Ltd to perform this play does NOT include permission to use any copyright music in the performance. The notice printed below on behalf of the Performing Right Society should be carefully read.

The following statement concerning the use of music is printed here on behalf of the Performing Right Society Ltd, by whom it was supplied
The permission of the owner of the performing right in copyright music must be obtained before any public performance may be given, whether in conjunction with a play or sketch or otherwise, and this permission is just as necessary for amateur performances as for professional. The majority of copyright musical works (other than oratorios, musical plays and similar dramatico-musical works) are controlled in the British Commonwealth by the PERFORMING RIGHT SOCIETY LTD, 29–33 BERNERS STREET, LONDON W1P 4AA.

The Society's practice is to issue licences authorizing the use of its repertoire to the proprietors of premises at which music is publicly performed, or, alternatively, to the organizers of musical entertainments, but the Society does not require payment of fees by performers as such. Producers or promoters of plays, sketches, etc., at which music is to be performed, during or after the play or sketch, should ascertain whether the premises at which their performances are to be given are covered by a licence issued by the Society, and if they are not, should make application to the Society for particulars as to the fee payable.

AUTHOR'S NOTE

The presentation of this pantomime should create no problem for the average drama group. The scenes alternate between full sets and lane scenes, thus allowing ample time for scene and costume changes. It has been specifically designed for production in the average hall, and obviously can be spread out to fill the largest theatre. As Dick Whittington is usually a very "male" orientated pantomime, opportunities for females are normally restricted to Fairy, Alice, and sometimes, the title role. In this version, I've tried to even things out more by replacing the usual Emperor or Sultan with a Sultana, and added the female slave Zubediah to replace a Vizier. Tommy can also be played by a female, and at a push, First Mate Starboard. The role of the Sultana however can easily revert to a male role by deleting two lines referring to her sex. Again, in the palace scene, if the Sultana is a good singer and it is decided to use her/him in the opening song, the Company song in the middle of the scene can be omitted. Songs for the production, not forgetting the dance and incidental music, should be bright and bouncy. Omit verses, and stick to the much better known chorus. As an old (very old) pantomime hand, may I advise a brisk approach, lots of smiles and positively overwhelming sincerity of characterization. Pantomime is FUN. Illogical, ridiculous, riotous and brash, but also beautiful and touched with pathos. What a young audience sees during your production can affect their theatre-going habits for the rest of their lives. Don't let them down.

Norman Robbins

ACT I

SCENE 1

Cheapside, London. 1377

A collection of timber and plaster houses in typical pantomime style, against a backdrop of old London. UR *is the frontage of Fitzwarren's Stores, with mullioned windows through which can be seen a variety of goods. There is a practical door. Other shops can be seen down* R *and* L. *It is a bright and sunny morning*

When the CURTAIN *rises, the Citizens of London are singing and dancing merrily*

Song 1 (Citizens)

At the end of the song, there is a flash, R, *and Fairy Bow-bells appears*

At once, all freeze in position as though turned to stone. She moves to just R *of* C *and speaks directly to the audience*

Fairy   London. Thirteen seventy-seven. A time of celebration.
The birthday of our Sovereign Lord,
King Edward—ruler of the Nation.
So join our merrymaking; your voices raise in song.
Rejoice. The King is still the King.

King Rat enters DL

Rat (*harshly*)   One moment, friend. You're wrong.

Fairy reacts in surprise

Old Edward sits on England's throne. With that I must agree . . .
But let me make it clear to all that London Town belongs to me.
Without my blessing, don't forget, no citizen grows fat.
They tremble at my very name.

Fairy   Begone, you foolish rat.
You think too highly of yourself. You're nothing but a pest.
A creature known as vermin, and a most unwelcome guest.

Rat (*snarling*) You'll rue the day you spoke those words.
I mean to prove my claim.
Soon all shall bow the knee to me
Or else *King Rat* is not my name.

Fairy (*amused*) King Rat indeed. Don't make me laugh.
Now kindly go away. We have no time to waste with
  you
On this, our special day.

Rat (*annoyed*) So be it, Fairy Bow-Bells ...
But from henceforth I swear
I'll use my evil powers to bring ruin and despair.

Fairy (*calmly*) You'd better not delay then
If that's what you hope to do.
To London Town there comes this morn
The youth who'll put an end to *you.*

Rat (*incredulously*) An end to me? A *youth* you say?
(*To the audience*) This fairy's gone quite mad.
She really thinks I'll fall a victim
To a simple country lad? (*He laughs harshly*)

Fairy (*sweetly*) No ordinary mortal he ...
But one both brave and kind.
Dick Whittington of Gloucestershire
Great fame and fortune here will find.
And in the centuries to come they'll tell the story true
Of how he rose to greatness and rid London Town of
  you.

Rat (*snarling*) You jest, of course. (*Aside*) And yet—and yet ...
I've often heard it said
"Fore-warned, one also is fore-armed." (*Thought-
fully*)
This Whittington is better *dead.*
(*To Fairy*) I'll seek him out. Destroy him.
Strike now, without delay.
I'll show you once and always that
King Rat o'er London *does* hold sway.

He laughs and exits L

Fairy (*sighing*) Oh, dear. Some people never learn.
He'll waste his time, I fear.
No harm will come to Whittington
As long as *I* am here.
(*Brightly*) So come. Ignore his foolish threats,
And join this happy throng. (*To the motionless Citi-
zens*)
Continue with your revels and
Sing out your joyous song.

She waves her wand and exits DR

The Citizens at once unfreeze, and there is a reprise of the opening song. At the end of this they form themselves into small groups and chat excitedly

As they do so, Alderman Fitzwarren enters from the inside of his store. He is elderly and a trifle vague, but warm and friendly. He sees the crowd and gives a delighted smile as he moves down C *and speaks to the audience*

Alderman Oh, I say. What a lot of people around this morning. Looks like we'll be having a busy day in the store. (*To Citizens*) Good-morning, everyone. (*He beams at them happily*)

Citizens (*brightly*) Good-morning, Alderman Fitzwarren.

Alderman Aha—you can't wait to get inside my little store, can you? Oh, we've got some wonderful bargains for you today. I just know you're going to be delighted with them. (*He ticks them off on his fingers*) There's see-through dresses ... for ladies who have to watch their figures. Combs without teeth—for bald-headed gentlemen. Tins of dog-food that taste of postman's leg—and a marvellous new knife that can slice four loaves of bread at the same time. We call it our four-loaf cleaver. (*He chuckles heartily at his own joke until he realizes that no-one else is amused and quickly sobers*) Ahem. Yes. Well—er—ahem. (*Briskly*) No pushing now. No pushing. Just form a nice orderly queue and we'll have everyone served in no time. (*He beams at them, happily*)

Girl But we haven't come here to shop, Alderman. We've come to watch the procession.

Alderman (*realizing*) Oh ... the *procession*. Yes. Yes. Of course. I'd forgotten all about *that*. (*He titters*) Silly old me. I'll be forgetting my own head next. (*He frowns*) Er ... *what* procession?

Man Haven't you heard? His Majesty, the King, is going for a sail in the Royal Yacht, and he'll be passing through Cheapside on his way to the Quay.

Alderman (*flustered*) Oh, my goodness. I'd no idea. Why didn't someone *warn* me? He may pop in for a box of his favourite sea-sickness tablets. (*To the audience*) I *am* by Royal Appointment, you know. (*Suddenly agitated*) We must get the store tidied up at once. Where's my assistant, Idle Jack? Has anyone seen him? (*He calls loudly*) Jack. Jack. Where are you?

Everyone looks about

Girl (*looking off* UR) Here he comes now.

Idle Jack enters UR. *He is a bright and chirpy individual, wearing dreadfully "loud" clothing. He moves down* C

Jack (*to the audience and Citizens*) Hiya, everybody. (*To Alderman*) Morning, Fitzy.

Alderman (*slightly indignant*) Don't you "Fitzy" me, young man. This is the third time this week you've been late for work. Don't you have an alarm clock at home?

Jack Course we do—but there's nine of us in our family and my Dad only sets it for eight.

The Citizens laugh as Fitzwarren reacts

(*Grinning*) No. I'm only pulling your leg, Fitzy. As a matter of fact, the *real* reason I'm late is because I was watching the early morning news on television, and it was all about your new ship, *The Saucy Sue.*

Alderman (*surprised*) Really? (*Beaming*) Ah, *The Saucy Sue.* My pride and joy. Cost over half a million pounds, you know. (*Interested*) What was it they had to say about her?

Jack Well—you know you sent her to Canada to pick up a cargo of yo-yos? (*He mimes working a yo-yo*)

Alderman (*nodding*) Yes. Yes.

Jack Well on the way back, she ran into a terrible storm and bumped into an iceberg.

Alderman (*horrified*) Oh, my goodness. She didn't *sink*, did she?

Jack (*nodding*) Yes. Ninety-nine times.

The Citizens laugh and exit

Alderman (*annoyed*) Oh, you wicked boy. I don't believe a word of it. Now into the store at once and tidy everything up. I want the whole place spick and span in case His Majesty decides to pay us a surprise visit. Is that understood?

Jack (*dismayed*) Eh? But—but—you don't expect me to do it on my *own*, do you? Not all that lot? It'll take me a week to wash the cheese slices. Can't Sarah give me a hand?

Alderman Certainly not. Sarah's my cook, not a shop assistant. And besides . . . a bit of hard work will do you good. You're the laziest person I've ever employed, and if I could only find someone trustworthy to replace you, I'd sack you on the spot.

Jack (*grinning*) Give over. You wouldn't do that, Fitzy. Not to *me*. Not *really*. (*Worried*) Would you?

Alderman (*sternly*) I certainly *would*. Now I'm off to the Guildhall for a very important meeting, and if everything's not in its place when I get back . . .

He leaves the rest of the warning unsaid and exits DL

Jack (*to the audience*) Oh, blimey. That's torn it. What am I going to do if he sacks me? I've had no training. I've got no skills, and everything I do ends up as a disaster. I'll probably end up having to be a planner for the town council. (*He sighs*) Oh, what a rotten start to the morning. I'm going to be depressed all day now. (*He thinks*) Here . . . just a minute though. I bet *you* could cheer me up, couldn't you? I'll tell you what to do. Every time I say "Ooh, I am fed up", will you all shout back, "Cheer up, Jack"? Will you do that for me? Will you?

Audience reaction

Oh, smashing. All right then. We'll have a little practice, shall we? (*He calls*) Oooh, I am fed up. (*He practises with the audience until he is satisfied with their volume*) That's great. I feel better already.

Sarah enters, from inside the store. She is a woman of unspecified age, wearing too much make-up and an outrageous cook's costume. She carries a large rolling pin

Sarah (*as she enters*) Who's making all that noise? Clear off, before I wrap this round your earholes. (*She waves the rolling pin then sees Jack*) Oh, it's you, is it? I might have guessed. (*She moves down to join him*)

Jack (*seeing her*) Hallo, Sarah. (*He gives her a nervous wave*)

Sarah (*tight-lipped*) Never mind "Hallo, Sarah". And what time do you call this, then, eh?

Jack (*groaning*) Oh, don't *you* start on me as well. I'm not *that* late. And anyway—I couldn't help it. Not this time. I had this dream you see. Last night. When I was asleep.

Sarah Oh, you sleep at home as *well* as in the shop, do you?

Jack (*ignoring the interruption*) I dreamed I had a ticket for the Cup Final at Wembley and there I was, watching it. (*All excited*) Cor. What a match. One goal each and only half a minute to go. (*His excitement increases*) Come on (*local team*).

Sarah (*grimly*) Never mind "Come on (*repeats name*)". How could dreaming about the Cup Final make you late for work?

Jack Well—they had to play extra time, didn't they?

Sarah (*wincing*) Oooh. Any excuse'll do, won't it? Any excuse. It's no wonder you're called Idle Jack. You're so lazy, whenever your nose runs, you stick it out of the window so the wind can blow it.

Jack (*protesting*) Give over. I'm not that bad.

Sarah Aren't you? Well what about yesterday morning, then? When I asked you to fill up the salt cellar for me? How long did *that* little job take, eh? How long did that take? *Six and a half hours.*

Jack Well, what did you expect? You can only get a few grains at a time through that silly little hole in the top.

Sarah (*to the audience*) Oooh. They put better heads than his on sweeping brushes. (*To Jack*) Now just you listen to me, bubble-brain. If you're not inside that store serving the customers by the time I count three, there's going to be trouble. Understand? (*She brandishes the rolling pin*)

Jack (*dismayed*) Ohhh, I hate serving. You know I can't add the prices up properly. I did all my training in (*local supermarket*). Can't you do it for me, Sarah?

Sarah (*bridling*) Me? You've got to be joking. The Royal Procession's coming this way in a few minutes and I want a good view. I'm going upstairs to put my best frock on, sit by the window and wave my hair. (*She pats her hair-do*)

Jack (*puzzled*) Eh? We've not sold out of flags, have we?

Sarah (*to the audience*) Oooh. And to think I once thought he was the answer to a maiden's prayer. (*Tartly*) It's no wonder girls aren't praying much these days, is it? (*To him*) Right, cloth-head. Into the store. And when you've got a few minutes to spare you can cut me a few slices of tongue for lunchtime.

Jack (*wrinkling his nose*) Tongue? Oh, I hate tongue, Sarah. I couldn't eat anything that's come out of an animal's mouth.

Sarah Oh, all right, then. You can have an egg. Come on. Inside.

Sarah and Jack exit into the store, chattering

As they do so, Dick Whittington enters UL. *He is a handsome, but poorly dressed youth, carrying his wordly possessions in a rough cloth bundle, tied to a stick, supported on his shoulder. He moves down* C, *looking around in wonder*

Dick London at last. How big it seems compared with the village of Pauntley where I was born. (*He sighs*) All the same, I'm starting to wish I'd never left Gloucestershire. What a fool I was to believe the stories everyone told me—that the streets of London were paved with gold. Why, they're just mud and cobblestones, exactly the same as back home. And the people. So very many of them—but not one with a kindly word for a penniless boy without a friend in the whole city.

There is a loud mewing off R, *and the clattering of tin cans*

(*Surprised*) What on earth's that?

Tommy the cat, comes hurrying on, R. *A length of string has been tied to his tail, to which has been attached several empty tins*

Tommy (*plaintively*) Mee-owww. (*He runs around trying to lose the cans*)
Dick (*concerned*) Oh, the poor creature. I've got to help him. (*He calls to Tommy*) Here, puss. Here.

Tommy goes to him

Of all the cruel tricks to play. (*He kneels beside Tommy*) Don't worry. I'll soon have you free. (*He unties the cans*) There. (*He stands and tosses the cans off-stage*) All gone.

Tommy rubs himself against Dick, purring loudly

(*Laughingly*) Oh, you don't have to thank me, Mr Cat. I'm only too pleased to have been of help to *someone*. Yours is the first friendly face I've seen since I arrived in London Town.
Tommy (*nodding*) Meow. (*He indicates himself*)
Dick (*surprised*) You mean *you've* just arrived here, too?
Tommy (*nodding*) Meow.
Dick So we're *both* strangers in the big City? Well in that case, allow me to introduce myself. Richard Whittington of Pauntley Court, Gloucestershire—(*he bows deeply*)—though most people call me Dick. And what might *your* name be, I wonder?
Tommy (*shaking his head*) Mee-owwww.
Dick (*surprised*) You haven't got one? But that's terrible. A handsome cat like you *has* to have a name. Let's see if I can think of one for you. (*He thinks*) How about—*Thomas*? What do you think to that?
Tommy (*shaking his head undecidedly*) Meow.
Dick (*disappointed*) No?

Tommy shakes his head again, then standing on his hind legs, whispers in Dick's ear

But you wouldn't mind if people called you *Tommy*. (*He laughs happily*)

Tommy drops down into a crouch again

Very well, then. That's it. From now on, you can be Mr Tommy Cat.

Tommy shows his approval

(*Ruefully*) Well . . . it's been very nice meeting you, Mr Cat—I mean—Tommy—but I'm afraid I'll have to be moving on. I've still to find a job and somewhere to live. (*He peers through the window of Fitzwarren's Store at the display*) Not to mention something to eat. (*Longingly*) Mmmm. What delicious looking food. If only I had some money. It's been two whole days since I ate last, and I'm absolutely famished.

Tommy scampers off DL *without Dick noticing*

There's cheese . . . and fruit . . . bread and cakes. (*Remembering*) Oh . . . but *you* must be hungry too, musn't you? (*He turns and sees Tommy has gone*) Tommy? (*He looks around*) Tommy? (*Sadly*) He's gone. Without even saying goodbye.

Tommy hurries back on again. He carries a large rat in his mouth

(*Delightedly*) You're back.

Scampering over to Dick, Tommy drops the rat

(*Surprised*) A rat?

Indicating it with his paw, Tommy points to Dick and rubs his own stomach

(*Realizing*) You brought it for me to *eat*? (*He laughs*) Oh, you clever creature. (*Hugging Tommy*) That's the kindest thing anyone's done for me since I left home. (*Ruefully*) But all the same, I'm afraid I can't eat a *rat*. I'll tell you what. You keep it for yourself and I'll wait a little bit longer. (*He yawns*) As a matter of fact, I think I'm more tired than hungry. Walking all night has quite worn me out. I wanted to get here early, you see. Perhaps I can rest outside this store. I'm sure the owner won't mind. (*He settles himself down at the side of the door and closes his eyes. Sleepily*) Happy eating, Tommy. (*He falls asleep*)

Tommy plays with the rat for a few moments, then accidently knocks it off-stage DR. *He exits after it*

The Lights dim

King Rat enters DL. *He sees Dick asleep and sneers*

Rat (*to the audience*) Is *this* the mighty Whittington
Who comes to steal my crown
And win the admiration of each soul in London Town? (*He laughs*)
Oh, no, dear Fairy Bow-bells . . .
Your plan will fail, I vow,
For as he sleeps, my chance I'll take
And strike him dead *right now*.

He advances towards Dick in a menacing attitude

With a loud spitting noise Tommy bounds on to the stage and faces him

Rat staggers back in fright as Tommy advances

> A cat. Ten thousand curses. For now I'll have to flee.
> (*To Dick*)
> But this I promise, Whittington ...
> You haven't heard the last of me.

He exits L, *hurriedly, chased by Tommy*

As they exit, Captain Port and First Mate, Starboard enter UR. *They are shabbily dressed and obviously down-at-heel. Moving past Dick without noticing him, they move down* C

Starboard (*eagerly*) Here we are, Captain. Right outside it. (*He indicates the store behind them*) Fitzwarren's Stores.

Port (*growling*) Aharrr. Belay there. Splice the mainbrace and shiver me timbers, yer scurvy dogs. Aharrrr. (*He screws up his left eye*)

Starboard (*blankly*) Eh?

Port (*glaring at him*) I said—Aharrr. Belay there. Splice the mainbrace and shiver me timbers, yer scurvy dogs. Aharrr. (*He screws up his left eye*)

Starboard Yes, I know. But what does it mean?

Port Mean? It don't mean anything, you idiot. *All* experienced sailors talk that way.

Starboard *I* don't.

Port (*pityingly*) Of *course* you don't, oyster-brain. But you're not an experienced sailor, are you? The nearest to a ship you've been is *hard*ship.

Starboard (*indignantly*) No it's not. Let me tell you, I was once the only survivor of a terrible shipwreck.

Port (*surprised*) Eh? How did you manage that?

Starboard I missed the boat.

Port (*wincing*) Ooooh. I might have expected a stupid answer like that one. It's no wonder Alderman Fitzwarren gave me the job as ship's Captain, and you only got the First Mate's position. Employers always prefer a brainy Captain.

Starboard (*disgusted*) Huh. I've got just as many brains as you have. *And* I know as much about sailing.

Port Oh, yes? All right, then. I'll test you. Suppose you were in Mid-Atlantic and facing South. What would be on your right hand?

Starboard Easy. My thumb and four fingers.

Port (*carried away*) Then suddenly a terrible storm blows up from the East. The waves are fifty feet high. What do you do?

Starboard Throw out an anchor. (*He tosses out an imaginary anchor*)

Port Then *another* storm starts in the West. The waves are a hundred feet high. What do you do now?

Starboard Throw out another anchor. (*He tosses a second imaginary anchor*)

Port But now an even worse storm comes from the North. The waves are six hundred feet high. What do you do *this* time?

Starboard Throw out some more anchors. (*He flings anchors in all directions*)

Port (*heavily*) Just a minute. Just a minute. Where are you getting all the anchors from?

Starboard The same place you're getting all the storms. (*He looks off* L) Ooh, look. A pretty girl coming this way. How about trying to steal a little kiss from her? (*He rubs his hands in anticipation*)

Port (*scornfully*) You bilge-swilling barnacle. A real sailor doesn't have to steal kisses. You can get them for nothing if you go about it the right way.

Starboard (*wide-eyed*) Can you?

Port Course you can. All you've got to do is *impress* the lady.

Starboard And how do we do that, then?

Port Easy. (*He smirks*) Just wait till she sees us dressed like this. Girls will do anything for a man in a uniform.

Starboard (*scornfully*) Give over. And anyway, we're not going to impress her in *these* uniforms. They're all worn out and dirty.

Port So what? All we've got to do is *act* like sailors and she'll hardly notice how scruffy we look.

Starboard I don't get you.

Alice Fitzwarren enters UL. *She is a very pretty girl and carries a small posy of flowers*

Port (*not noticing*) Stand like this. (*He adopts a stance*) *Show* her you're naval.

Starboard at once hoists his shirt to display his navel. Alice gives a little scream of surprise

(*Startled and noticing Starboard*) No, you fathead. Not your bellybutton navel. Cover it up. (*He tugs Starboard's shirt back into place*)

Alice (*uneasily*) Who are you?

Port (*swaggering*) Percival Port, ship's Captain, at your service. (*He bows awkwardly*)

Starboard And First Mate, Sidney Starboard. (*Admiringly*) Cor ... you aren't half pretty, miss. How about a kiss for two lonely sailors?

Alice (*surprised*) I beg your pardon?

Port You heard. One little kiss each, and you'll make us the happiest men in London Town. (*He puts his arm around her*)

Alice (*indignantly*) Certainly not. Let go of me at once.

Starboard (*grinning*) Not till you've given us a kiss.

Port attempts to kiss Alice who struggles

Alice (*calling*) Help. Help.

Dick awakens and sees the struggle

Dick What? (*He springs to his feet and hurries down*) How dare you? (*He grabs Port and swings him round*) Take that.

Dick strikes Port, who howls and staggers back, releasing Alice

And that.

He hits Starboard, who also howls

Port and Starboard quickly exit

(*To Alice*) Are you all right, miss?

Alice (*relieved*) Yes, thank you. (*She smiles*) I'm sure they meant no *real* harm, but I'm very glad you came along. (*She frowns*) Excuse me for asking, but aren't you a stranger to these parts? I haven't noticed you before and I thought I knew most people in Cheapside.

Dick (*smiling*) Yes. I only arrived in London this morning. Allow me to introduce myself. Dick Whittington of Gloucestershire. (*He bows*) Here to find fame and fortune.

Alice And I'm Alice Fitzwarren. (*She drops a small curtsy*) My father owns the store behind us.

Dick In that case, he must be the happiest man in all London. Not only does he own its finest store, but the most beautiful girl in the City has to be his daughter.

Alice (*amused*) Why, thank you, Master Whittington, but there are many girls prettier than I am in London Town.

Dick I rather doubt it. But even if it *were* true, I may not be here long enough to find out. Unless I find a job and somewhere to live, I'll have to return to Gloucestershire.

Alice (*quickly*) Oh, there'll be no need for that. If I ask him, I'm sure Father would give you a job. And as for somewhere to live—why—you could live with *us*. Inside the store.

Dick (*eagerly*) Do you mean that? Honest and truly? (*Delighted*) Oh, what a *wonderful* day this is turning out to be after all. Who cares if the streets of London *aren't* paved with gold? I've made two good friends already *and* found myself a job.

Alice *Two* friends?

Dick Why, yes. You and Tommy—a rather handsome cat I met up with just a short while ago.

Alice A cat? Oh, I *love* cats. Do let me see him. Please.

Dick (*frowning*) I'm not sure ... (*Looking off* L) Ah. Here he comes now.

Tommy comes strolling on L

Alice (*delightedly*) Oh ... isn't he *beautiful?*

Dick (*to Tommy*) Meet my new friend, Tommy. Miss Alice Fitzwarren.

Tommy (*politely*) Me-oww. (*He stands up and bows*)

Dick I'm going to work in her father's store. Isn't that marvellous?

Tommy (*nodding*) Meow. (*He indicates himself*) Me-oww?

Dick (*amused*) What's that? You'd like to work there too? (*Doubtfully*) Well—I don't know. (*He looks at Alice questioningly*)

Tommy turns to her and puts his paws together in supplication

Alice (*laughing*) Of course you can. (*To Dick*) He can keep the store free of rats and mice. Just give me a few moments. I'll go in and arrange it all with Father.

She exits into the store

Dick (*delightedly*) Oh, Tommy. Our luck's changed at last. The curtain's about to rise on a brand new life for both of us. Thanks to Alice Fitzwarren, everything's coming up roses. (*Shouting*) Yippee.

Song 2 (Dick)

At the end of the song, the scene ends

SCENE 2

A quiet street

Jack enters R *looking downcast. He wears a white apron over his costume*

Jack Oooh, I am fed up.

Audience reaction

Here, I'll tell you what. I aren't half glad to get out of that store for a few minutes. Everybody's been picking on me this morning. I've been in so much hot water, I feel like a tea-bag. Talk about *complaints*. They've never stopped since I arrived. One woman came in and moaned about the dust on the counter-top. "Look at it," she said. "That counter hasn't been cleaned for at least six months." I said "Well, don't blame me, missis. I've only been working here a fortnight."

Alderman enters L

Alderman (*a trifle annoyed*) Aha. Caught you. Idling again. What did I tell you only an hour ago? (*Sternly*) I've a good mind to hire *another* assistant right this very minute.

Jack Cor. I wish you would. We'd get a lot more done in that store if there were two of us, you know.

Alderman (*spluttering*) Oooooh. What are you doing out here? Why aren't you inside, serving the customers?

Jack (*thinking furiously*) Ah ... well ... there's a very good reason for that, Fitzy. As a matter of fact, I've just been doing my good deed for the day.

Alderman Good deed?

Jack Yes. I looked out of the window and saw this little old lady stood standing on the pavement with all her shopping bags, and as there was so much traffic about, I thought I'd better help her across the road.

Alderman (*mollified*) Oh, I see. Well, in that case ...

Jack I mean—it's all good for the store's image, isn't it? And I haven't been away more than twenty minutes.

Alderman (*startled*) Twenty minutes? How could it have taken twenty minutes to help an old lady across a road?

Jack Well—she didn't want to go.

Alderman (*annoyed*) Ooooooh. Now that's enough. From now on, you're not to set foot outside the store during working hours—under any circumstances. Do I make myself clear?

Jack (*protesting*) But ... but ... what if there's a phone call for you, and you're standing out here on the pavement?

Alderman In that case, just *call* me, you idiot.

Jack Oh, I couldn't do that, Fitzy. I know you're absent-minded, but I'd never call you an idiot.

As Alderman reacts, Sarah enters R, *looking concerned. She wears another exotic gown*

Sarah (*spotting them*) Oh, thank goodness I've found you in time. (*To Alderman*) You'd better watch out. There's a couple of funny looking fellers hanging around outside the store, and they say they're waiting for *you*.

Alderman (*worried*) Oh, dear. I hope they're not after money. Business has been terrible lately, and I'm overdrawn at the bank. (*To Sarah*) They haven't got bills, have they?

Sarah No. Just noses, like everyone else.

Alderman (*remembering*) Ah, of course. (*Relieved*) It'll be my new Captain and First Mate. I advertised for them in the (*local newspaper*) and the letter they sent said they'd be arriving today. I'm putting them in charge of my favourite ship, *The Pickled Herring*.

Sarah (*surprised*) Eh? I wouldn't trust either of them with *my* ship, if I had one. They've been drinking.

Jack Oh, give over, Sarah. All sailors like a drink now and then.

Sarah I know. But these two are so drunk, they're dropping pennies down a drain and looking up at Big Ben to see if it's got their weight right.

Alderman Good gracious. Perhaps I'd better go and speak to them. (*To Jack*) And as for you, my lad, back into the store at once. There may be customers waiting.

He exits R

Sarah (*to Jack*) Well. You heard the man. Off you go. (*She preens herself*)

Jack What about you? Aren't you coming?

Sarah Certainly not. Now I've seen the Royal Procession, I'm going down to Buckingham Palace to watch them changing the Guard.

Jack (*groaning*) Oh, no. They've not dirtied their uniforms *again*, have they?

Sarah (*wincing*) Ooooh. (*To the audience*) I don't think *he'll* ever need to worry about having brainstorms. He'll be lucky to manage a *light drizzle*.

Jack (*indignantly*) Here. Less of the nasturtiums. I'm not as daft as I look, you know.

Sarah (*tartly*) Well that's something to be thankful for, isn't it? Listen, Big-ears. If you were as bright as you think you are, you'd be on your bended knees right now, asking me to marry you.

Jack (*startled*) Eh? But I've only known you two weeks. Why would I want to marry *you*.

Sarah Well, it's obvious, isn't it? If I were your wife, I'd be able to share all your worries and problems.

Jack (*puzzled*) But I haven't got any worries and problems.

Sarah (*patiently*) I know that, stupid. I'm talking about *after* we were married. And besides—I'm a smashing cook. Remember that chicken I roasted for dinner last night? I bet *that* tickled your palate, didn't it? (*She smirks*)

Jack Not half. You'd forgotten to pull the feathers off it. Oh, I couldn't marry *you*, Sarah. I couldn't marry anybody. I'm too poor. In fact, the last time I had *measles*, I could only afford to have one spot.

Sarah (*frowning*) Well what do you do with your wages? Don't you ever save anything?

Jack Course I do. I had a fortune in the bank till last week, and then I had to spend it all on my brother's funeral. (*He sniffles sadly*)

Sarah (*surprised*) Brother's funeral?

Jack (*nodding*) Yes. He fell off some scaffolding and died. (*He sniffles again*)

Sarah (*blinking*) But you told me your brother was a roadsweeper. What was he doing on scaffolding?

Jack They were hanging him.

Sarah (*annoyed*) Ooooh. I might have expectorated something like that from you. Now stop messing about. Are you going to propose to me, or aren't you? Because if you're not, I shall have to start thinking again about marrying (*she names a famous pop singer*).

Jack (*impressed*) I didn't know (*repeats name*) had asked you to marry him.

Sarah He *hasn't*. But I've thought about it before today. And besides—I don't want you to be broken-hearted if somebody else carries me off. (*Archly*) After all, you're not the only feller in London chasing after me, you know. Only last month I refused to marry one chap, and he's been hitting the bottle ever since. (*She smirks and preens*)

Jack Blimey. That's carrying a celebration a bit far, isn't it?

Sarah glares at him

I'll tell you what, Sarah. I'll think about proposing to you on one condition.

Sarah (*suspiciously*) What's that?

Jack You give me a hand in the store instead of going to watch the soldiers.

Sarah (*trapped*) Oh, all right, then. But remember. If I don't get a proposal before tonight, there's going to be trouble. Come on. Back to the store.

Jack and Sarah exit R

As they do so, King Rat enters L*, panting heavily and in a temper*

Rat(*snarling*)   Confound that interfering cat.
                              My plans all came to naught.
                              Young Whittington remained unharmed,
                              (*Incredulously*) Whilst *I*, King Rat, was almost caught.

(*Menacingly*) But come tonight he'll breath his last
I give you all my word.

Fairy enters R, *un-noticed by Rat*

                    (*Roaring*) I'll prove King Rat is Lord of all.
Fairy   (*pityingly*) How utterly absurd.

Rat spins around to face her

                    I've told you once already that your time is running
                    out.
                    Your day is done, I'm glad to say, however loud you
                    shout
Rat   Don't count your chicks before they hatch. The
                    game's not over yet.
                    A lesson harsh, I mean to give, and one you won't
                    forget.
                    Once Whittington is dead, I vow you'll rue your
                    intervention.
                    To bring the *plague* to London Town shall be my firm
                    intention.
Fairy (*sadly*)   Your idle threats are typical of any cornered rat.
                    Despite your powers, you'll never harm
                    Dick Whittington and Thomas Cat.
                    You'll quickly find that they're a match for any tricks
                    you try.
                    So do your worst, my foolish friend. Good day to
                    you.

Fairy exits R

Rat (*snarling*)   Goodbye.
                    (*To the audience*) I'll very soon wipe off the smile
                    From that one's simpering face.
                    She'll find that I possess, in full,
                    The cunning of my ancient race.
                    (*He glances off* R) But here he comes. I must away,
                    My evil plans to make. (*He sneers*)
                    To rid myself of Whittington
                    Will be a piece of cake.

He laughs harshly and exits L

Dick, Alice and Tommy enter R

Dick (*moving* C) Oh, Alice, I don't know how I'll ever be able to thank you
enough. I've only been here a few short hours, and already I've got a job
and somewhere to live.
Tommy (*indicating himself*) Meowww.
Dick (*laughing*) And that goes for Tommy, too.
Alice There's no need for thanks. Really, there isn't. (*She sighs*) To tell you
the truth. I'm not even sure how long the job's going to last. Father may

have to sell up his business, you see. All the profits are being eaten away by mice and rats, and our customers get fewer every day.

Dick Don't worry, Alice. Once Tommy starts work, there won't be a rat in London dare show his face inside the store. And who knows—maybe *I* can come up with an idea or two for improving business?

Alice If only you could. I don't know what will happen if we *do* have to close down. The store means more to Father than anything else in the world.

Dick (*smiling*) I somehow doubt it. If *I* were your father, the most precious thing in the world to *me* would be *you*.

Alice Oh. (*Slightly embarrassed*) It's very kind of you, Dick, but I don't know how you can say that. After all, we've only just met and you hardly know me.

Dick (*nodding*) That's true, but sometimes you don't have to know a great deal about someone to realize how much they mean to you.

Alice (*surprised*) And do *I* mean something to *you*?

Dick Strangely enough, you do. (*Quickly*) Oh, I'm not saying it's love— though it *could* be. And I'm not saying it's because you're so beautiful— though you *are*. It's just that—well—with you here beside me, I feel that at long last there's a real reason for being alive.

Song 3 (Dick and Alice)

At the end of the song, the Lights fade to a Black-out as Dick, Alice and Tommy exit casually

Scene 3

Inside Fitzwarren's Store

A shop interior. A backdrop depicts rows of shelving, laden with assorted goods. Centre of the store, almost up against the backdrop of it, a battered old safe stands. (This is simply a painted hardboard box with a practical door and an interior shelf.) Several children's shoe-boxes (empty) are in evidence on the counter top

When the scene begins, a group of children are performing a lively dance watched by several customers and Sarah, who stands DL

Dance (Children)

At the end of the dance, the adults applaud and one of the ladies steps forward to speak to the children

Lady Well done, children. Very good indeed. Now is everyone happy with their new shoes? No pinched toes or rubbing heels?

Children (*brightly*) No, Miss Clatterclogs.

Lady (*relieved*) Good. (*To Sarah*) In that case, we'll take them *all*. Send the account to my dancing school, if you please. (*To the children*) Come along, children.

She ushers the children out

Sarah (*fondly*) Oh, doesn't it take you back? (*She moves* C) I remember when I used to dance like that. Well—not exactly like that. I was more of what you might call a *novelty* dancer. (*She simpers coyly, then thinks on*) You do know what a novelty dancer is, don't you? Well, let me explain it to you. A novelty dancer is someone who does these very exotic routines, wearing nothing but a smile and two coats of gold paint. (*She demonstrates some exotic movements*) Mind you, I didn't do it for long. The novelty wore off. Here ... but you'll never guess what they used to call me. (*Proudly*) "The Queen of the Roaring Twenties." (*She smirks*) There was nobody could Charleston faster than I could, and the Mayor's eyes popped out like Chapel hat-pegs when I showed him my Black Bottom. (*Her eyes sparkle at the memory*)

Woman (*frostily*) Excuse *me*. When you have *quite* finished your idiotic chattering, I'd like to be *served*. (*She glares at Sarah*)

Sarah (*aside: grimly*) Yes. On a big silver plate with an apple rammed in her cake-hole. (*To the woman; sweetly*) So sorry, madam. I'll attend to you now. (*She bustles to behind the counter and tidies the boxes*) May I help you?

Woman (*snootily*) I want three slices of best bacon. And don't forget to make them lean.

Sarah Certainly, madam. Which way? (*She chortles with laughter at her own wit, but quickly recovers*) Lean bacon, lean bacon. (*She glances around*) Ah, yes. Here it is. (*She reaches under the counter, produces a slab of mouldy-looking bacon and blows the dust off it*)

The customers react

Woman (*shocked*) Ugh. I couldn't possibly buy *that*. It looks as though flies have been laying eggs on it.

Sarah (*scornfully*) Don't be daft. Flies wouldn't go near *this*. I spray it with (*she names a popular flykiller*) every morning.

The customers react again

Woman (*horrified*) Ohhhh. I shall never set foot in this place again.

She sticks her nose into the air and exits, followed by the rest of the customers

Sarah Snooty old faggot. (*She replaces the bacon under the counter*) Still, now I've got rid of that lot, I've just got time for a nice cup of tea and a few minutes rest. (*She chuckles*)

Tommy bounds on to the stage L

Aghhhhhhh. It's a monster moggy. (*Waving her apron at him*) Shoo. Shoo. Go away. Shoo.

Fitzwarren, Dick and Alice enter L

Alice *(amused)* It's all right, Sarah. There's nothing to be afraid of. He only wants to be friendly.

Sarah Yes. Well he can go and be friendly somewhere else. *(She notices Dick)* Oooh. *(Quickly she tidies herself)* I didn't know we were expectorating visitors. *(She eyes Dick with interest)*

Alderman *(shaking his head)* No, no, Sarah. They're not visitors. This is our new shop assistant, Dick Whittington, and that's Tommy his cat.

Dick *(gallantly)* Good-morning, Miss Sarah. I'm very pleased to meet you. *(To Tommy)* Come and say hallo, Tommy.

Tommy crosses to Sarah and rubs himself against her, curling himself about her skirts

Sarah *(pleased)* Oooh, I say. I think he's taken a fancy to me. *(She strokes him)* It's either that, or he can smell my new perfume. Essence of Kit-E-Kat.

Alderman Now then. I want you to take very good care of them, Sarah, and see they get plenty to eat. *(To Dick)* She makes a lovely stew, my boy, and her dumplings are the biggest in London.

Sarah *(smoothing her bust and simpering)* Flatterer. *(To Dick)* Well ... er ... Why don't you pop into the kitchen a bit later on? There's going to be dozens of things for lunch.

Alderman Really? *(He rubs his stomach with anticipation)*

Sarah Yes. I'm opening up a tin of baked beans. Here ... and seeing as how this is a special occasion ... I'll try out that new recipe I found in this week's "Woman's Own". Colgate pie.

Alice *(puzzled)* Colgate pie???

Sarah Yes. You mix toothpaste in with the pastry so it cleans your teeth while you're eating, and you don't have to brush them afterwards. *(She simpers)* See you later.

She beams and exits DL

Alderman *(clearing his throat)* Well, let's get down to business, my boy. Come along with me and I'll tell you exactly what it is you have to do. *(To Alice)* Won't be long, my dear.

Fitzwarren and Dick exit UR

Alice *(delightedly)* Oh, Tommy. Everything's working out exactly as I'd hoped. I just *know* you're both going to be happy here. *(She pauses as though deciding something)* And shall I tell you something else?

Tommy *(interested)* Meowww.

Alice *(motioning him to come closer)* Promise you won't tell anyone.

Tommy comes closer, sits up, and crosses his heart

It's going to make *me* happy too. You see—for the very first time in my life ... I think I'm in *love*.

Song 4 (Alice)

At the end of the song, Alice and Tommy exit UR

As they do so, Idle Jack enters DR

Jack (*to the audience*) Oooh, I am fed up.

Audience reaction

Huh, it's all right for you lot, but what about *me*? Now this Dick Whittington's working here, I'm going to be out of a job. And to think that only last week I invented a new health food so old Fitzy could make his fortune. I've got a smashing name for it, as well. It's called "Rise and Shine". I made it out of yeast and furniture polish.

Alderman enters UR

Alderman (*seeing Jack*) Aha. Caught you unaware, have I?

Jack (*startled*) Eh? Caught me *what*?

Alderman Unaware. Unaware. (*Sternly*) You know what unaware is, don't you?

Jack Course I do. It's my vest and Y-fronts.

Alderman (*wincing then trying again*) Why is it every time I walk into the store, I catch you standing here doing nothing?

Jack (*helpfully*) Perhaps it's because you've got rubber soles on your shoes and I can't hear you coming.

Alderman (*annoyed*) Now just you listen to me, young man. If things don't improve around here, I'm afraid you and I will have to part company.

Jack (*dismayed*) Oh, don't say that, Fitzy. Things'll get better. I know they will. (*Kindly*) Besides—where would you go?

Alderman (*exasperated*) Oooooooh. I wouldn't go anywhere. *You*'ll be the one to go. You'll be out of a job and Master Whittington will be my chief assistant. Now make yourself useful whilst I go to see when our new safe will be ready. With the lock broken on our old one, anyone could open it up and steal the takings. (*Sighing*) I can't *wait* for the Twentieth Century to come along so someone can invent the credit card.

Alderman exits DL

Jack (*to the audience: amazed*) Well, I'll be pasteurized. Fancy wanting to sack *me* and give my job to that Dick Whittington. He's only been in the place two minutes. (*He thinks*) Here—hang on, though. Perhaps if I get him into trouble, Fitzy'll get rid of him instead of me. That's a good idea, isn't it, kids?

Audience reaction

Captain and Mate enter UL

Port (*to the audience*) Belay there, yer swabs. Batten the hatches and lower the mainbrace. (*To Jack*) What's all the noise about, matey?

Jack (*looking them up and down*) Who are you?

Port Captain Port and First Mate Starboard of the good ship *Pickled Herring.* (*Grandly*) Sailing on the morning tide to an exotic place where smiling dark-eyed people in bright silk clothing spend their lives breathing warm, moist air, delicately scented with fragrant spices.

Starboard (*blankly*) I didn't know we were going to the (*local curry centre*).
Port (*pushing him*) Idiot. I'm talking about *China*. The Mysterious East.
Jack (*impressed*) Cor. *I've* always wanted to go to China. (*Very interested*) Here—is it really as mysterious as everybody says?
Port Mysterious? I'll say it's mysterious. (*He drops his voice*) Very strange people, the Chinese are. Do nothing all day but drink gallons of *tea*.
Jack Well what's mysterious about that? *We* drink gallons of tea over here.
Port Yes. But we drink ours out of *cups*, don't we? In China they drink it *out of doors*.

Jack reacts

Starboard (*drawing Jack closer*) And guess what happens to all the thieves and robbers they catch in China? They cover 'em with sand and cement and turn them into solid lumps of concrete.
Jack (*wide-eyed*) What do they do that for?
Starboard So's everybody can see they're *hardened criminals*.

Port and Starboard chortle with laughter

Jack (*realizing his leg is being pulled*) Oh, stop messing about. I'm not in the mood for joking. I'm going to get the sack, I am. (*Sulkily*) Now do you want something, or don't you?
Port Well, seeing as how we were passing, like, we thought we'd come in and collect something special we've ordered for the voyage. Save you the trouble of delivering it. But never mind about that. Why's old Fitzwarren going to sack you?
Jack (*disgusted*) Huh. It's all that Dick Whittington's fault. Him over there, tying up that parcel. (*He indicates off,* UR) Wormed his way in here ten minutes ago, and now he thinks he can run the place. Oooooh. If only I could get rid of *him*, Fitzy'd *have* to keep me on.

Port and Starboard look off UR

Starboard (*startled*) Cap'n. It's him. The feller that bashed us about this morning.
Port Stap me vittals. You're right. (*To Jack*) Tell you what, matey. We've got an old score to settle with him ourselves. If the three of us gets our heads together, maybe we can get him the sack instead of you. Now listen to this . . .

They huddle closely and whisper secretly. They then straighten and attempt to look innocent as . . .

Dick enters UR, *carrying a medium-sized box wrapped in brown paper, tied with string and marked "Fragile"*

Jack Oh, hallo. You must be Dick Whittington, the new assistant.
Dick (*smiling*) Why, yes. I am. And you must be Jack.
Jack That's right. And this is Captain Port and First Mate, Starboard.

They leer at him

Dick (*wryly*) Yes. We've met already. As a matter of fact——

Jack (*interrupting*) You weren't going somewhere with that parcel you're holding, were you? I mean—you weren't going out with it?

Dick Well, yes, I was. Alderman Fitzwarren told me to take it to——

Jack The Post Office, I expect. He sends everything through the post, you know.

Dick Really?

Jack But *I* wouldn't take it there if I were you. Not a parcel marked "Fragile" like that one.

Dick Well, perhaps not, but——

Jack It'd never get where it's going in one piece, you see. (*He takes the parcel*) First of all they'd stamp it—like this. (*He bangs his fist hard on the top*) Then they'd drop it into a sack on the floor—like this. (*He drops it onto the floor*) And everyone who goes by would kick it—like this. (*He kicks the box across the shop*) Oh, no. I wouldn't take it to the Post Office.

Dick looks at the box in horror, then runs to pick it up as the others grin and smirk

Dick But ... but I wasn't taking it to the Post Office. I wasn't going anywhere *near* the Post Office. (*He comes back shaking the box which rattles with the sound of broken glass and metal*)

Starboard (*in mock horror*) Oh, don't tell us you were going to send it by rail! Thank goodness *we* were here to warn you. (*He takes the box from Dick*) If you send a parcel like this by rail, they'll drop it on to a weighing machine like this. (*He drops it heavily on to the floor*) Then they'll jump up and down on it to see if it's well packed—like this ... (*He jumps up and down on the parcel*) And then they'll kick it on to the platform like this ... (*He kicks it across the shop*) And somebody else throws it on to the train. Oh, I wouldn't send anything fragile by rail.

Dick moves slowly over to collect the parcel as the others smirk and snigger

Dick (*coming back with the battered parcel*) But you don't understand. I wasn't going to send it by rail. Alderman Fitzwarren told me to——

Port Send it by *sea*, I suppose. (*With horror on his face*) Oh, you should never send a parcel by sea. (*He takes the box*) First of all it's dropped into the hold—like this. (*He hurls it to the floor*) And all the other parcels are dropped on top of it ... like this. (*He jumps on the parcel*) And when the ship begins to roll it's thrown to one side—like this. (*He stoops, snatches up the parcel and throws it* L) And then to the other side—like this. (*He hurries* L, *snatches up the parcel and throws it* R) And by the time it gets to where it's going, whatever's inside it is smashed to pieces. Oh, no. I'd never send a parcel like that by sea.

Jack, Port and Starboard snigger

Dick But I wasn't going to. Alderman Fitzwarren told me to take it down to the docks and deliver it to *you*. It's the portable TV set you ordered this morning.

The trio react in dismay and there is a snap Black-out

All exit in darkness

A green follow-spot reveals King Rat, DL

Rat (*hissing*) In sewer deep, beneath the streets,
For hours I've sat and schemed . . .
Fine plans for Master Whittington
Within my brain have teemed.
But all of them are useless if I can't get past his cat . . .
How dare it thwart the will of *me*—His Majesty, King Rat?
But wait—perhaps there *is* a way. Yes, yes. I see it now.
Tomorrow morn will see the back of Whittington—I *vow*.

With a laugh of triumph, he exits DL

The follow-spot vanishes and the Lights come up to half. Dick is tiredly sweeping up the floor with a besom. UR. *His stick and bundle rest against the wall* R. *Tommy is playing with a ball of wool by the counter. Fitzwarren is behind the counter adding up the cash*

Alderman (*counting coins*) Thirty-seven, thirty-eight, thirty-nine pounds and five pence. (*Surprised*) My goodness. This is the most money we've taken in months. You've certainly brought us luck, young Whittington. (*He begins to put the money in a small sac*)

Dick (*pausing in his sweeping*) Oh, it's nothing to do with me, sir, but it certainly did get busy in here this afternoon. (*He resumes sweeping*)

Alderman (*kindly*) Now, now, Dick. No need for modesty. You've worked very hard—which is more than I can say for Idle Jack. He's so lazy, he could fall asleep running for a bus.

Dick (*smiling*) Don't be too hard on him, sir. He *is* trying to do better. He borrowed a book from the shelf this afternoon. *How to cure laziness.*

Alderman Yes. I know. He asked Sarah to read it for him. Now finish your sweeping, and as soon as I've put this in the safe, (*holding up the sac*) I'll have supper sent in for you.

Dick That's very kind of you, sir, but to tell you the truth, (*he yawns*) I'm so tired I don't think I could eat a thing. And besides—I've eaten more today than I have all week. (*He yawns again*)

Alderman Well—if you're quite sure . . . (*He opens the safe, puts the sac inside, then closes the safe again*) Then I'll just say good-night and wish you both pleasant dreams. There's a bed made up for you behind the counter. Sleep well, Dick. Night-night, Tommy.

Tommy waves good-night

(*Beaming*) Oh, I can't *wait* to tell Alice how well we've done.

He exits delightedly, UR

Dick (*propping the besom against the wall*) Well, that's it, Tommy. The end of our first day in London. (*He yawns*) I don't know about you, but as far as I'm concerned, it's been one of the happiest of my life. I can hardly wait to see what tomorrow brings. (*He yawns*) I think I'll sleep in *front* of the counter, tonight, though. That way I'll be able to make sure no-one tries to steal the takings. (*He sinks to the floor in front of the counter and yawns again*) Good-night, Tommy. See you in the morning. (*His eyes close*)

Tommy stretches, then as the Lights begin to dim, he prowls around the store finally curling up DR. *Waving good-night to the audience, he falls asleep. The Light continues fading until the store is in semi-darkness*

In a green follow-spot, King Rat appears DL

Rat (*contemptuously*) Enjoy your dreams, young Whittington.
For soon you'll come to grief.
From London shortly you'll be gone;
Disgraced, and branded as a thief.
I'll prove to threaten me was
Fairy Bow-bells' big mistake.
But now, my plan I'll carry out
And vanish ere these fools awake.

Moving to the safe, he opens it and takes out the money sac. Holding it aloft for everyone to see, he closes the safe again then crosses to Dick's bundle and thrusts the sac inside it

The deed is done. When comes the morn,
For missing coins they'll search,
And find them hidden in this bag—which leaves Dick
Truly in the lurch.

He gives an evil laugh and exits DL

The Lights fade to a complete Black-out, then at once begin to brighten again, continuing up to full. Outside the store, a handbell is rung loudly and a voice calls

Man (*off, distantly*) Eight o'clock on a fine sunny morning, and all's well. (*Closer*) Eight o'clock on a fine sunny morning, and all's well.

Both Dick and Tommy stretch and awake

(*Fading*) Eight o'clock on a fine sunny morning and all's well.
Dick (*jumping to his feet*) Oh, my goodness, Tommy. We've overslept. The shutters should have been taken down half an hour ago. I'd better do it right away and open the doors. I may just have time for a quick wash before the first customers come in.

He hurries off UL

Tommy quickly begins to wash himself, licking his paws and cleaning his face and whiskers

As he does so, customers pour into the shop, all eager to buy and chattering excitedly

Alderman Fitzwarren hurries on DR

Alderman (*startled*) Good heavens. The place is packed already and we've only just opened. (*Calling*) Sarah. Alice. Come quickly. (*Moving* CF)

Sarah and Alice hurry in to join him

Alice What is it, Father? (*She sees the crowd*) Oh.

Sarah What's happening? (*She looks around*) Blimey—I've never seen so many happy faces. Has somebody shot an Income Tax Collector?

Alderman No, no. This is all young Whittington's doing. (*Delightedly*) I *knew* I was right to hire him. Where is the lad? Has anyone seen him?

Alice (*looking off* UL) Here he comes now.

Dick enters

Alderman (*grabbing him and pumping his hand*) Dick, my boy. How on earth did you do it? No, no. Don't tell me. Just let me thank you from the bottom of my heart. You've saved us from almost certain bankruptcy.

Song 5 (Alderman, Alice, Sarah and Chorus)

At the end of the song, everyone congratulates the bewildered Dick

Dick Well, thank *you*—but——

Alderman (*interrupting*) No time to talk just now. We've a shopful of customers waiting. You begin serving whilst I get the money out of the safe.

He hurries to the safe and opens it as Dick, Sarah and Alice begin taking orders

(*With a loud gasp*) It's gone. The money's gone.

Everyone (*shocked*) Gone? (*Everyone looks at each other in dismay*)

Sarah We've been burgled. Somebody's cracked the crib.

Dick But that's impossible. No-one's been here but *me* until a few minutes ago.

Alderman (*most concerned*) Oh, dear. How very awkward. In that case, I'm afraid I'll have to ask you to empty your purse, Dick.

Alice (*shocked*) Surely you don't think *Dick* stole the money?

Alderman (*helplessly*) I don't know *what* to think, Alice. All I know is that the money was there last night and now it isn't.

Dick It's all right, Alice. Of course I didn't steal the money. I wouldn't steal anything. (*He slips his purse off his belt*) Here you are, sir. As you can see, it's absolutely empty. (*He hands it over*)

Jack enters DL, *rubbing his eyes*

Alderman (*relieved*) He's right. There's not a penny in it.

Jack What's the matter? What's going on?

Alice Oh, Jack. Someone's robbed the safe and taken all our money.

Jack Eh? Does that mean we won't get paid? Oh, I am fed up.

Audience reaction

I bet it's him that's taken it. (*He glares at Dick*)

Sarah (*indignantly*) Here. Watch who you're accusating, you. We've already looked in his purse, and there's nothing in it but fresh air.

Jack Ah ... but have you looked in that bag of his? The one over there that's tied to his stick. (*Indicating it*) He could have hidden it in that, couldn't he?

Dick Don't be ridiculous. There's nothing in there but a clean shirt. But you're very welcome to examine it.

He gets the stick and bag and returns C, *followed by Tommy. He hands them to Fitzwarren who puts his hand inside the bag and pulls out the money sac. Everyone gasps with surprise and looks at Dick*

Alderman (*hurt*) Whittington. How could you? (*He drops the stick and bag*)

Alice (*dismayed*) Dick.

Dick (*protesting*) But—but—I didn't put it there. Alice—everyone—you've got to believe me.

Jack Oooh. I knew we wouldn't be able to trust him. Right from the minute he walked in here.

Alderman (*to Dick*) I'm sorry, Whittington. I had high hopes for you, but after this ... (*He shakes his head sadly*)

Dick (*helplessly*) But sir—I'm innocent. I didn't steal your money. I don't know how it got into my bag.

Jack No. But we do. (*To the others*) Don't we?

Chorus Thief. (*They glare at Dick*)

Alderman I think you'd better go, Whittington. We don't want you here any more.

Dick (*desperately*) Why won't anyone *believe* me?

Tommy pulls at his arm and indicates himself, but Chorus look away

Alice (*moving to him*) *I* believe you, Dick. Of course you didn't steal the money. It's all a terrible mistake.

Sarah Yes. And I don't think he did it either. You've only got to look at him to tell he's not a thief. He hasn't got a black mask, a striped jumper, *or* a sack marked "swag". (*She pauses*) And he's got lovely legs.

Alderman I'm sorry, but my mind's made up. He's the only one who *could* have done it. (*To Dick*) Leave this shop at once.

Dick I know how it must seem, sir, but I swear I'm innocent and one day I'll prove it. (*To Alice*) Goodbye, Alice. Perhaps when I return to London, we'll meet again. (*He picks up his stick and bag*)

Alice But where are you going?

Dick Who knows? I suppose we'll just have to follow the road outside.

Sarah (*dabbing at her eyes*) Oh, I don't think that'll do you any good. I've been working here twenty years, and I've never seen it move yet.

Dick (*to Tommy*) Come along, Tommy. It's time we were leaving.

Dick moves off UL, *followed by a downcast Tommy and exits*

Sarah and Alice comfort each other as the Lights fade to a Black-out for the end of the scene

SCENE 4

On the way to Highgate

Fairy Bow-Bells enters R

Fairy
Although it seems that boastful Rat's
Succeeded in his aim
To rid himself of Dick and Tom . . .
I'll spoil his little game.
To London Town they shall return;
(Their task's yet uncompleted.)
And though he plays a thousand tricks,
By them, "King Rat" shall be defeated.

She exits

Port and Starboard enter L

Starboard (*groaning*) Oooh, what are we doing out here in the countryside? We've been walking for miles and me feet are killing me.

Port Oh, stop complaining. You *know* why we've come out here. It's so we can have a private chat without being overheard. (*Glancing around*) This looks a likely spot. Not a soul in sight.

Starboard Well make it quick, will you? I want to visit my sister before the ship sails. Her husband was fixing the television aerial last night and slipped off the roof.

Port Eh? Was he hurt bad?

Starboard No. But he would have been if he hadn't fallen through an open manhole into the sewer and drowned.

Port slaps him with his hat

Port Idiot. Now listen. We're going to be in real trouble if anyone finds out we've never sailed a ship before. The closest to water *we've* ever been, is a rowing boat on the Serpentine.

Starboard Yes—but I did have a cousin once who died on a ship. They had to bury him at sea, and it was a terrible tragedy. Half the crew drowned trying to dig his grave.

Port (*wincing*) Oooh. (*He pulls Starboard closer*) Come here. Now just suppose somebody says they feel sea-sick? What do we have to do?

Starboard We don't have to do anything. They'll do it on their own. (*He mimes being sick*)

Port (*hitting him again*) Oh, I don't know why I bother. Here I am—trying to keep us out of trouble, and all you can do is make stupid jokes.

Starboard Well—I don't know what you're worried about. There'll be nobody on board except us and the crew. We can leave everything to them, can't we?

Port (*realizing*) Hey . . . you're right. I never thought of that. We can just sit in my cabin and watch the latest videos until we get to where we're going. Here—I hope it won't be cold, though. I can't stand cold weather and my feet get frozen.

Starboard Oh, you don't have to worry about that. Take a hot water bottle with you.
Port (*shaking his head*) Wouldn't work. I'd never get my feet through the little opening in the neck.

Sarah and Jack enter. Jack's arm is in a sling

Sarah (*delightedly*) Aha. Just the fellers we're looking for.
Port Eh? (*He notices Jack*) Here—what's happened to *you*, shipmate?
Jack Oooh, I am fed up.

Audience reaction

We were trying to catch up with you on my supersonic skateboard and I fell off and bashed my nose.
Starboard Well why have you got your arm in a sling?
Jack I'd look pretty daft with my nose in one, wouldn't I?
Sarah Oh, shurrup. (*To Captain and Mate*) Now listen, you two. We've got a message for you from Alderman Fitzwarren. He's decided to close the shop for a fortnight and take a month's holiday.

Jack takes off the sling and stows it in his pocket

Port What's that got to do with us?
Sarah Well—he said to tell you that he and Alice are going with you on the voyage, and not only that—he's asked *us* to come along too. (*She beams delightedly*)

Port and Starboard look at each other in dismay

(*To the audience*) Oooh, girls. You should see the new bikini I'm going to wear. I'm not saying it's small, but if a moth got into it, it'd die of starvation. Still—you've got to be fashionable, haven't you? And if anybody makes a criticism, I shall just shrug it off.
Port Here—hang about, missis. Hang about. We can't be taking passengers on *The Pickled Herring*.
Starboard What if we run into a storm and sink? Can you swim?
Jack Course we can swim. (*Smugly*) *I'm* a champion diver.
Sarah Yes. Only last night I found him in a dive in Soho.
Port Ah—but you might have to swim long distances if anything *did* happen. Could you *do* that? (*Importantly*) Me and Starboard could swim from this spot here, right over to that church steeple in the distance (*he indicates the back of the theatre*) if we had to.
Jack (*disbelievingly*) Don't be daft. Even Tarzan couldn't do that.
Starboard Why not?
Jack There's no water.
Sarah Anyway—never mind about swimming and things. Fitzy says we're all coming with you, so you'd better get used to the idea. (*Excitedly*) Oooh, just think—first thing tomorrow morning we'll be sailing into the sunset for the holiday of a lifetime. (*Remembering*) Here—and we'd better pack some costumes for the Fancy Dress Ball, as well.
Port What Fancy Dress Ball?

Sarah The one we have on our last night at sea, whenever we go on a cruise.

Port and Starboard look blank

Oh, I've been to dozens of them. I remember one year I caused an absolute sensation when I went as a native girl in a hula-hula skirt. There were so many fellers wanting to dance with me, I had to make 'em draw straws. It was a good job it was a warm night. (*She simpers*)

Port (*not too happy about it*) Well—if we've got to take you, we've got to. But it won't be a holiday, you know. You'll have to help with all the work.

Jack (*dismayed*) Oh, I knew there'd be a catch in it.

Sarah (*shrugging*) Well—it doesn't bother me. As a matter of fact, I'm already trying to decide what we can have for our first meal on board.

Starboard Here—how about some caviare? I've always fancied a bit of that.

Sarah (*doubtfully*) Oh, I don't know about caviare. It's very expensive. (*Thinking*) But I'll tell you what. I'll give you a plateful of tapioca and a pair of dark glasses. You'll never know the difference.

Jack I know what *I'd* like, but I'll have to do without 'em, until we get back to London again.

Sarah What's that?

Jack The tastiest meal that's ever been put before the British public. A great big bagfull of me uncle's fish and chips.

Port (*delightedly*) Ahaaar. (*He rubs his hands with glee*) Now yer talking.

Song 6 (Jack, Sarah, Port and Starboard)

At the end of the song, there is a Black-out for the end of the scene

SCENE 5

The top of Highgate Hill

The backdrop is a rural view as seen from the top of Highgate Hill, and is flanked by stately oaks. A grassy knoll is UR, *and a milestone is embedded in this, indicating "5 miles to London"*

Dick enters UL, *tired and footsore. His stick is across his shoulder*

Dick Five miles from London and a hundred more to travel before we reach Pauntley. (*Moving* CF *and sighing deeply*) Who'd have thought two days ago, I'd be on my way home again this morning? (*Glancing round*) Tommy? Tommy—where are you?

Tommy limps on UL, *his downstage paw held off the ground*

Tommy (*pitifully*) Meowww. (*He sits down and dangles his paw*)

Dick (*dismayed*) Oh—you're hurt. (*He drops his stick and bundle, and hurries to Tommy. Kneeling beside him, he takes hold of the paw*) Poor Tommy. Let me see. (*Examining it*) Ah—here we are. It's a big thorn.

We'll soon have that out. It may hurt a little, though.

Tommy covers his eyes with his free arm

Here we go. (*He pulls out the thorn*)
Tommy (*pained*) Meowwwwwwwww. (*He clutches his paw and dances around*)
Dick (*startled*) I'm sure it didn't hurt *that* much.

Tommy nods firmly

Oh. (*Contrite*) Well, I'm very sorry. But it's all gone now. (*He stands again and throws the thorn away*) Perhaps we can walk a few more miles before we stop for lunch. What do *you* think?

Tommy shakes his head

(*Surprised*) "No"?
Tommy Meoww. (*He shakes his head and rubs his stomach*)
Dick Oh. You mean you're hungry *now*?

Tommy nods vigorously

So am I. But a crust of stale bread and a lump of mouldy cheese is all we have, and it's got to last until we can beg something else.
Tommy (*miserably*) Meowwww.
Dick (*relenting*) Oh, all right. I don't suppose it makes any difference. Once it's gone, it's gone. Come on, we'll sit on that bank over there.

Dick picks up his stick and bundle, and he and Tommy move to the bank and sit. Dick opens the bundle and takes out a small piece of cheese and a tiny crust of bread

Here you are, Tommy. You have the cheese and I'll have the bread.

They eat the food in a single mouthful

Well—that didn't take long, did it? (*He sighs*) We'd better start walking again.
Tommy Meow. (*He shakes his head*)
Dick But we can't sit here all day.
Tommy (*waving his "thorn" paw miserably*) Meowwww.
Dick (*concerned*) Still hurting, is it?

Tommy nods unhappily

Perhaps I'd better wrap it up for you? (*He takes out his handkerchief and wraps the paw*) There. Is that better?
Tommy (*shaking his head*) Meow. (*He attempts to flick the wrapping off*) Meowwwww.
Dick Don't do *that*. It's to stop the dirt getting in.

Tommy shakes the wrapping more vigorously

(*Warningly*) Tommy. (*He stands and moves downstage*)

Tommy glances at him, then attempts to shake off the wrapping unseen by Dick. These attempts are continued during the following speech

(*Looking out front*) How beautiful London looks from here. I wonder if I'll ever see it again? Cheapside. Fitzwarren's Store. *Alice.* (*Sighing deeply*) If only I knew who put the money in my bag. I'd go straight back there and——(*He breaks off*) Oh, what's the use? Almost everyone thinks I'm a thief and I don't suppose they'd listen to me for a moment. That's really the thing that hurts most, you know. If I had *one* wish, I think it would have to be that I could prove to everyone I was absolutely innocent.

Tommy has given up with his struggle and curls up on the knoll as . . .

Fairy Bow-bells enters DR *unseen by either of them*

Fairy Your wish, young Richard Whittington, will very soon be granted.

The Bells of London Town, by me, this day have been enchanted,

And even now begin to stir in ev'ry steeple tall;

A message true to send to you. Hark. Hear their distant call.

She waves her wand and exits

The sound of bells is heard (to the tune of "Oranges and Lemons"). At first they are faint but increase in volume as Dick speaks

Dick (*turning towards the sound*) Listen, Tommy. It's the bells of London. And all ringing together. What on earth can it mean?

Chorus (*off* L; *softly*) Turn again Whittington,
Fortune awaits you.
Come back to London
And you'll be Lord May'r.

(*Louder*) Turn again Whittington,
Come back to London.
Fortune awaits you
And you'll be Lord May'r.

Dick (*amazed*) Those voices. What's happening? (*Looking round*) Tommy. Wake up.

Chorus (*off; full
voice*) Come back. Good fortune
Awaits you in London.
Sir Richard Whittington
Four time Lord May'r.

(*Fading*) Turn again Whittington,
Fortune awaits you.
Come back to London
And you'll be Lord May'r . . .

The voices die away but the bells continue to ring softly for another stanza before ending

Dick (*dazed*) I must be dreaming. How could a poor boy like me become Lord Mayor of London? It's absolutely impossible. And yet—I heard it. I really heard it. (*To the audience*) Do *you* think I should go back to London?

Audience reaction

Do you?

Audience reaction

Then I *will*. (*He hurries upstage to the knoll*) Wake up, Tommy. Wake up. We're going back. (*Determined*) We're going back to London.

As Tommy begins to wake, Dick sings the last four lines of the opening song

At the end of the song, the Junior Chorus enter in red and black military uniforms with busbies and perform a spirited march or tap routine, whilst Dick exits UR *with Tommy*

Dance (Juniors)

As the Juniors exit at the end of the routine, the Senior Choristers enter in Coster outfits, laughing and joking. At once they launch into a rousing Coster song in which the Senior Dancers join with gusto. If desired, Fitzwarren, Alice, Sarah, Jack, Port and Starboard may also take part, wearing similar costumes to the Chorus

Song 7 (Choristers)

At the end of the song, the Chorus part to allow Dick to enter up CB *wearing Guildhall Finery, and accompanied by Tommy*

A musical reprise of the opening number is played as they move CF, *then everyone joins in a full-throated reprise of the last four lines of the song. At the end of the song, the Main Tabs are brought in for the scene end and Finale of Act I*

CURTAIN

ACT II

SCENE 1

The Quayside

The entire rear wall is occupied by the bulk of "The Pickled Herring", and a short flight of stone steps lead to a gap in its side for entering or leaving the ship. To the R, a picturesque Ship's Chandlers is situated, and to the L, "The Beaux Legs Inn". Both have practical doors

When the CURTAIN *opens, Sailors are dancing a merry Hornpipe, whilst Citizens stand watching and clapping in rhythm*

Dance (Sailors)

At the end of the dance, everyone resumes their business, chatting, loading the ship, etc., and as they do so ...

Alderman Fitzwarren enters DL, *followed by a sad-looking Alice*

The Chorus gradually exit during the following dialogue

Alderman Come along, Alice. Come along. We mustn't be late for the sailing. (*He sees the ship and beams with delight*) Ahhh, here we are. My very own *Pickled Herring*. (*To Alice*) I'd better find the Captain right away and check that all our luggage has arrived.

Alice Do we *have* to go with them, Father? I'd much rather stay here in London.

Alderman (*gently chiding*) Now, now, Alice. I know you're still upset about what happened yesterday, but it's over and done with now. A nice little cruise on *The Pickled Herring* will give us all a chance to forget how cruelly Master Whittington deceived us.

Alice (*protesting*) But he *didn't*, Father. I *know* it. Dick wasn't a thief.

Alderman (*regretfully*) I must admit—I can hardly believe it myself. But the money *was* found in his possession, so what else *could* I do but dismiss him?

Alice (*earnestly*) I'm not *blaming* you, Father. I just thought if we stayed at home, perhaps we could find out who the *real* thief was and clear Dick's name.

Alderman (*gently*) Oh, Alice. I know you mean well, but even if Dick *was* innocent, it's too late to do anything about it now. We don't even know where he went. No. I think the best thing to do is pretend that we never met the boy, and leave it at that. Now come along. We'd better get aboard. I'm sure you'd like to see your cabin before we sail.

Alice (*downcast*) Not just yet, Father. If you don't mind, I'd rather stay here and wait for the others to arrive.

Alderman (*sighing*) Oh, very well, then. But don't forget to call me the moment they do. I want to make sure they've both got their passports.

He ascends the steps and boards the ship, exiting R

Alice Oh, I'm so miserable. How can I possibly enjoy myself when I know an innocent person is being blamed for something he didn't do? Poor Dick. If only I knew how to find him. Perhaps between us we could *prove* he didn't steal that money.

Fairy Bow-Bells enters DR

(*Surprised*) Oh.

Fairy   Your faith in young Dick Whittington
         Will bring you great reward;
         And though, for now, things may look black,
         His fortunes soon will be restored.
         Within the hour, I promise you,
         He'll clear his tarnished name,
         And with the help of Thomas cat,
         Defeat "King Rat" and win the game.

Alice I don't understand. Who *are* you? And who's King Rat?

Fairy   Just call me "Friend". As for "King Rat" ...
         That villain was the thief
         Who stole your father's money and
         Caused all of you such grief.
         But now to London, Dick returns
         His purpose to fulfill;
         To find great fame and fortune,
         And with *both* our help, he will.

Fairy exits

Alice (*calling*) Wait ... (*She hurries* DR) She's gone. (*Dazed*) I must have been dreaming. But she seemed so real. And the things she said. (*Moving* C) Oh, if only it were true. (*Thinking*) But what if it *is*? What if this King Rat *did* steal the money and put the blame on Dick? (*Excitedly*) I must tell Father at once.

She hurries up the stairs on to the ship and exits R

Sarah enters UL *in a bit of a state, and totters down* CF *with a sigh of relief*

Sarah (*panting*) Oh, girls. I've just had a terrible experience. (*Glancing around to make sure she cannot be overheard*) I've been followed. By a feller. All the way down the street. I walked ever so slowly but he wouldn't catch up. Anyway—I got so worried, I went up to a policeman and complained. "There's a man following me," I said. "I'm sure he's drunk." Well the policeman looked me up and down and said, "Yes. I think he must be." Mind you—*he* was just as bad. Offered to walk part of the way with me if I'd give him a little kiss. Cheeky monkey. "Come on," he said.

"I bet if it was Christmas, you'd give me a kiss under the mistletoe." I said "You must be joking. I wouldn't kiss you under chloroform, mate." And you'll never guess what happened then. He looked me straight in the eye and offered me fivepence for one. *Fivepence. (Indignantly)* Oooh, I was so furious. *Fivepence.* I mean—what kind of a girl did he think I was. Fivepence for a kiss. *(Absentmindedly she puts her hand in her pocket and gives a loud shriek)* Aaaaaaaah. *(She scrabbles about inside her pocket then relieved produces a coin)* Oooh, I thought for a minute I'd lost it.

Idle Jack enters UL

Jack *(to the audience)* Ooh, I am fed up.

Audience reaction

Morning, Sarah. *(He comes down to her)* Sorry I'm late, but I went to Chalk Farm for some milk and I had to lend a hand with the animals and things.
Sarah How do you mean, lend a hand?
Jack Well, the sheep were too hot, so I got some shears and cut all the wool off for them. And after that, one of the horses hurt his leg so I put his harness on and pulled his cart for him—then just as I was leaving, I found two of the hens were poorly.
Sarah Oh, yes? And what did you do for *them*? Lay all the eggs? *(Tartly)* Ooooh. You've got an excuse for everything, you have. It's no wonder you're not married yet. If it wasn't for me, no girl would look at you twice.
Jack Give over. Only this morning a couple of nice girls smiled at me.
Sarah I'm not surprised. The first time *I* saw you, I laughed out loud.
Jack Oh, come on, Sarah. Don't let's start the holiday with an argument. Give me a big smile. Go on. Smile for Jack.
Sarah *(after thinking about it)* Oh, all right, then. *(She simpers)*
Jack *(staring at her closely)* Here—do that again.
Sarah *(surprised)* Eh?
Jack *(eagerly)* Do it again. What you did just then.
Sarah You mean—smile? *(She gathers herself and simpers again)*
Jack *(staring at her in disbelief)* It is. It *is. (He chortles with glee)*
Sarah *(flustered)* What is? What's wrong?
Jack Nothing. It's just that when you smile like that. You look just like my favourite film star.
Sarah *(preening)* Ooooh. *(She simpers again)* You mean *(she names a famous beauty)*?
Jack No, no. Daffy Duck.
Sarah *(annoyed)* Ooooooh. That's done it. That has *done* it. Just for that, you can find somebody else to marry. I'm fed up of playing around with a penniless shop assistant. From now on, I'm going to play for bigger stakes. I'll marry a butcher.
Jack Oh, I was only pulling your leg, Sarah. I didn't mean it.
Sarah Yes you did. You can't pull the wool over *my* thighs. *(Firmly)* If you want to marry me now, you'll have to woo me and pursue me for a change. Show me a bit of romance.

Jack You mean—you want me to do something daft like singing soppy love songs under your bedroom window?

Sarah Well—that'd do for a start. And I could lean out and throw a beautiful red rose at you.

Jack In a moment of mad passion, I suppose?

Sarah (*grimly*) No. In a five-kilo plant pot. (*To the audience*) Oh, girls. Don't they make you want to spit? The fellers today, they haven't got a scrap of romance in 'em. If only they were all like that (*she names a famous screen lover*). Ooooooooooooh. (*Her eyes cross in ecstasy*)

Jack (*repeating the name with a sneer*) What's so special about *him*?

Sarah I'll tell you. Last night I only *dreamed* about him, but he wined me and dined me, took me out dancing for half the night then drove me home in his white Rolls-Royce and escorted me to the door. Then he put his arms around me and kissed me and cuddled me and squeezed me so tightly I could hardly breath. And after *that*—well—I woke up.

Jack (*disgusted*) Huh. I don't think that's anything to get excited about.

Sarah Maybe not. But tonight I'm going to bed early so I can find out what he's going to do next. (*She rubs her hands in gleeful anticipation*)

Jack Oh, give over, Sarah. What do you want to go dreaming about folks like him for when I'm around? (*Sticking his chest out*) I'm a *real* man, I am. I've got hairs on me chest.

Sarah Yes. And so has Lassie. (*Tartly*) Listen sunshine. The sort of man *I'm* looking for is one who'll treat me like a queen.

Jack In that case, I've got the very man for you.

Sarah Who's that?

Jack King Henry the Eighth.

Song 8 (Sarah and Jack)

At the end of the song, Alderman Fitzwarren and Alice appear UR

Alderman (*calling*) Sarah. Jack. Everyone. Come quickly. Oh, my goodness. What have I done? What have I *done*?

As he and Alice hurry down the steps . . .

Citizens, Sailors, etc. enter curiously

Whittington was innocent. We must find him at once and beg his forgiveness. Search the entire city. I'll give a hundred pounds to the person who brings him back.

There is a reaction from the crowd, followed by a cry of alarm as . . .

King Rat appears DL

Sarah Blimey. It's (*she names an unpopular politician*)

Rat   Hold fast. Should any foolish soul attempt to claim that prize
              By seeking Master Whittington—I give my word—he dies.
              It was *my* scheme that drove him out—you'd best remember that

Before you dare to interfere with dealings of King
Rat.

Alice (*stepping forward*) You repulsive creature. How dare you let Dick be
blamed for *your* stealing?

Rat   Be silent girl. And watch your tongue or else I'll strike
you down.

That simpleton stood in the way of me e'r ruling
London Town.

But now we'll see no more of him—thanks to my
cunning scheme.

Dick Whittington is far away and I'll fulfill my dream.
(*He laughs*)

Dick enters DR

Dick Did someone mention my name?

There is a general reaction

Alice (*relieved and delighted*) Dick.

Alderman (*overcome*) Whittington, my boy. Thank goodness you've come
back.

Dick What's happened? (*He sees King Rat*) And who's that?

Alderman The villain who *really* stole the money from my safe so that *you*'d
get the blame. He's just admitted it.

Dick (*astounded*) What? But why? (*He looks questioningly at Rat*)

Rat   Don't play the innocent with *me*. I know your little
game.

You'll never live to see me die—as sure as *King Rat* is
my name.

My strength is of a hundred men: my heart devoid of
pity.

And this I vow—I'll kill you *now*—then evermore rule
London City.

All react but Dick

Dick Fine words, my repulsive friend, but I think a punch on the nose will
do you a world of good. (*He brandishes his fists*)

Alice (*calling*) Dick. Be careful.

Sarah (*to Jack*) Quick. Go get him some boxing gloves and put a good luck
piece inside one of 'em.

Jack What sort of good luck piece?

Sarah A dirty big horseshoe.

Dick and Rat face up to each other

Rat   In eagerness to breath your last, all caution to the
winds you cast.

You stand no chance against my might. By *magic* I
shall win this fight.

(*He lifts his arms to cast a spell*)

The watchers react in fear, but as they do . . .

With a loud meow, Tommy springs on to the stage DR, *facing King Rat in a menacing position*

> Ahhhh. (*Recoiling*) That cursed cat again. Once more I'll have to flee.
> With all my powers, against that brute I'm *still* as helpless as can be.
> But don't think that I'm beaten for I'll give you a promise true,
> When least expected, I'll return and put an end to *all* of you.

He exits quickly DL

Everyone relaxes

Alice He's gone. (*She runs to Dick*)
Dick (*embracing her*) Thanks to Tommy.
Jack Three cheers for Tommy the cat. Hip hip——

All cheer loudly as Tommy unconcernedly begins to wash

Alderman (*coming forward*) Dick, my boy. Can you ever forgive me for doubting you?
Dick (*generously*) Of course I can, sir. I'm only too pleased to know my name's been cleared.
Alderman You must come back to the stores as soon as we return from our holiday. And not only that—I'll increase your wages to sixpence a week. (*To the audience*) Well—this *is* six hundred years ago, remember.
Alice Oh, father. Couldn't Dick come *with* us? There's plenty of room on board.
Alderman Why not? (*To Dick*) What about it, my boy? Do you fancy a sea cruise?
Dick If all my friends are going to be with me—then there's nothing I'd like better.

Song 9 (Dick and Company)

At the end of the song, the scene ends in general rejoicing

Scene 2

In the shadow of a warehouse

Port and Starboard enter R, *hastily*

Port Hurry up. Hurry up.
Starboard I am doing. I am.
Port (*halting* C) Now wait. Wait. You're sure you haven't forgotten anything?

Starboard (*halting*) Course I'm sure. (*He ticks off on his fingers*) One pair of kitchen scales—for weighing the anchor. One pair of knitting needles and a ball of wool—for casting off. And one box of peppermints—for raising the wind. (*He hiccups*) Pardon.

Port (*glaring at him*) Never mind about that lot. What about the maps?

Starboard (*blankly*) Maps?

Port For showing us the way to where we're going, barnacle brain.

Starboard (*easily*) Oh, you don't have to worry about *maps*, Cap'n. *I* can direct us to where we're going. It's dead simple.

Port The only thing simple around here is you. How can *you* tell me the way to where we're going when you don't even know what *shape* the world is?

Starboard (*indignantly*) Yes, I *do*. It's square.

Port (*astounded*) Square?

Starboard Yes. You've heard of the four corners of the earth, haven't you?

Port Listen blockhead. What shape are your girl-friend's *ear-rings*?

Starboard Square.

Port No, no. I mean the ones she wears for best—on Sundays.

Starboard Oh. Round. She wears round ones on Sundays.

Port (*patiently*) Exactly. And the world is the same shape as your girl-friend's ear-rings.

Starboard (*light dawning*) Ohhh. I see. Square on weekdays and round on Sundays.

Port (*hitting him*) Ooooooh, you're as thick as pudding, you are. Didn't you ever go to school?

Starboard School? We went to *university*—me and my brothers. My older brother was reading Law, and my younger brother was reading History.

Port And what were *you* reading?

Starboard Gas meters. (*He chortles*)

Port (*wincing*) Were you born stupid, or did you have to practise?

Starboard I'm not stupid. I've got brains I haven't even used yet. Only last week, I was counting the pigeons in Trafalgar Square, when a feller came up to me and told me I was breaking the law, and if I didn't give him a pound for every pigeon I'd counted, he'd have me put in jail. So I put me hand in me pocket and gave him ten pounds. (*He smirks*)

Port (*amazed*) You did *what*? (*He groans*) Now I know you're crackers. He was pulling your leg, you dope. Having a joke with you.

Starboard Oh. Well—maybe he was, but the joke was on him in the finish.

Port (*baffled*) How do you mean, "the joke was on him"? You gave him *ten pounds*, didn't you?

Starboard Yes. But I told him a lie, didn't I? (*Smirking*) I'd actually counted a *hundred* pigeons.

Port Oooh. If somebody came along right now and tried to sell you the Tower of London, I think you'd be daft enough to buy it.

Starboard (*scornfully*) No I wouldn't. (*Pleased*) I bought it last night.

Port You bought the *Tower of London* last night? How much did it cost you?

Starboard My life savings. Two hundred pounds.

Port looks at him in disbelief, then begins to laugh. After a few seconds,

Starboard begins to laugh with him. For a few moments they shriek hysterically then Port sobers

Port Well I don't know what *you're* laughing at, you idiot.
Starboard *I* do. I got five hundred pounds for it this morning from *your* wife.

With a howl of rage, Port chases Starboard off L, *and there is a Black-out for the end of the scene*

Note: if more time is needed for the scene change, an extra song may be added at this point for Port and Starboard

SCENE 3

On board "The Pickled Herring"

The deck of "The Pickled Herring". When the scene begins, the deck is crowded with crew members, who sing a rousing sea-song as they swab it down with long-handled mops. Several buckets are also in evidence

Song 10 (Chorus)

At the end of the song, the crew exit casually with their cleaning things as . . .

Alderman Fitzwarren staggers on LC *looking very ill. He is followed by a concerned Sarah, in an outrageous costume*

Alderman Ooooooooh. (*He totters* C *and clutches his stomach*) Ooooooooooh.
Sarah (*alarmed*) Here. They've just cleaned this. You can't be sick here.
Alderman (*weakly*) That's what you think. Oooooh. (*He dashes for the side and leans over*) Oooooooooooh.
Sarah (*to the audience*) Oh, it's the same every year. The first few days at sea and he's sick all over the place. I've even tried putting glue on his porridge to see if it would help keep it down, but it doesn't seem to have done much good. And the problems we've had with him this morning. He was so bad, he sat down in a green chair and we lost him for an hour. (*She crosses to Alderman and taps him on the shoulder*) Here, I say . . . Fitzy. Would you like me to serve lunch up here in the open air? We're having stewed tomatoes, bacon, scrambled eggs and fried bread.
Alderman (*weakly*) No, thank you, Sarah. Just throw it over the side. It'll save a lot of time.
Sarah (*concerned*) Oh, you poor thing. (*She escorts him down* CF) Why don't you lie down and try those tablets the doctor gave you. He said they'd work wonders on your stomach.
Alderman I know. But they don't. Every time the ship rolls, they slide off.
Sarah (*to herself*) I wonder if he'd feel better if I distracted him? I'll give it a try. (*Pointing*) Oooh, look Fitzy . . . another ship.
Alderman (*miserably*) I don't want to see another ship. Call me when you see a bus. Oooooooooh.

Jack enters L, *limping*

Jack Oooh, I am fed up.

Audience reaction

Sarah What's the matter with *you*?

Jack I've been washing me trousers in the sink.

Sarah Eh? (*Puzzled*) Why didn't you use that beautiful modern top-loading washing machine in the laundry room?

Jack I tried, but every time I got into it, the paddle slapped my legs black and blue.

Sarah (*to the audience; wearily*) It's at moments like this when I actually start to believe in reincarnation. Nobody could be as stupid as he is in one lifetime. (*To Jack*) Look after Fitzy for a few minutes while I go find the feller in charge of this thing.

Jack Oh, the Captain's forward.

Sarah *Is* he? (*Simpering*) Well, this *is* supposed to be a pleasure trip.

Port and Starboard enter L, *behind her*

Port Avast, behind.

Sarah (*indignantly*) Who has? (*She turns to him*)

Port (*looking round*) Gather round, me hearties. I wants every one of the passengers here on deck. Come along now. Shake a leg. Jump to it.

Fitzwarren weakly totters down to join them

Dick and Alice enter R

Now then, me buckos. It's time for a bit of lifeboat drill.

Sarah Lifeboat drill? Oh, I don't think there's any need for that.

Starboard Oh, yes there is. It says so in the rule book. I mean—what would you do if you woke up in the middle of the night and found the ship had sprung a leak?

Jack Put a bucket under it and go back to sleep.

Port No, no. You don't understand. Just imagine it. (*With great drama*) The ship's *sinking*. We're all doomed. In a few minutes we'll all be dead.

Alderman (*fervently*) Thank goodness for that. (*He rushes upstage and leans over the rail again*) Oooooooooh.

Alice and Dick hurry up to him

Port Right, First Mate. (*He tries to look impressive*) Hand out the swabs.

Starboard 'Ere, 'ere, Captain.

Port (*shaking his head*) Ay, ay.

Starboard Pardon?

Port (*heavily*) Ay, ay.

Jack (*loudly*) Conga.

Jack and Sarah and Starboard form a conga line and do an impromptu dance, singing loudly

Port (*annoyed*) Quiet.

Sheepishly they halt

Starboard hurries off and returns with six long mops

Dick, Alice and Fitzwarren come back downstage and Starboard hands mops to them all but Port, retaining one for himself. Port moves DL *to observe*

Now then—form a line. Hurry, hurry, hurry.

The six form a ragged line. From R *to* L *the order is Sarah, Fitzwarren, Jack, Starboard, Dick, Alice*

Close up. Close up.

Sarah at once drops her swab and hoists her skirts to show gaudy bloomers. The others react

(*Anguished*) No, no. Not that way.

Sarah Oh. You mean *this* way? (*She turns her back to him and shows her rear*)

The others react again

Port As you were. As you were. (*He glares at Sarah*)

Sarah turns round again and drops her skirts

(*Heavily*) When I say close up—I don't mean *clothes* up—I mean close up. (*Angrily*) Stand closer together.

At once the two ends move sharply C, *trapping Jack and Starboard. They struggle to free themselves and Jack is pushed out of the line. Failing to get back in, he rushes* L *and stands next to Alice*

Squad—number.

Sarah One.

Alderman (*weakly*) Two.

Starboard Three.

Dick Five.

Alice Six.

Jack Four.

Port Who said that? Who said that?

Jack Who said what?

Port (*loudly*) *Four.*

They drop their swabs, duck and cover their heads with their arms

(*Baffled*) What are you doing? What are you *doing*?

Jack There's some idiot playing golf out here. Didn't you hear him shout "Fore"?

Port That was *me*, you fathead. There's no idiot out there playing golf.

Jack Left your clubs at home, did you?

Port As you were. As you were.

Everyone gets to their feet again, retrieving their swabs and returning to their original positions

(*Glaring at Starboard*) You stand at the end of the line.

Starboard moves to the end of the line, looks at Alice, then returns to his original position without Port noticing

Now then, from the right, number.

Sarah One.

Alderman Two.

Starboard Three.

Jack Four.

Dick Five.

Port Just a minute. Just a minute. (*He glares at Starboard*) I thought I told you to stand at the end of the line?

Starboard You did. But when I went, there was somebody there already, so I came back again.

Port (*furious*) Fall out. Fall out.

Starboard (*turning to Dick*) Hey, fish-face. You're the ugliest feller I've ever seen in my life. (*To Jack*) And you'd give a warthog nightmares.

Dick, Starboard and Jack tussle

Port Stop that. Stop it. What are you doing?

Starboard (*surprised*) You told me to fall out, didn't you?

Port Yes. But not with them, you fathead. As you were. As you were.

The line straightens again and Sarah rolls her eyes at someone in the front row and begins to mutter bitterly to them about the Captain's behaviour therefore missing the next command

Now then—we'll try it again. From the right—number.

Alderman (*weakly*) Two.

Jack Four.

Starboard Six.

Dick Eight.

Alice Mary at the cottage gate.

All (*dancing about*) Eating cherries off a plate. Two, four, six, eight.

Port (*furious*) As you were. As you were.

They all quickly resume positions except Sarah, who is still grumbling. Port glowers at her, then advances and taps her on the shoulder. She turns in surprise

Am I interrupting you?

Sarah I was just telling this woman——

Port (*screaming*) I'm not interested in what you were telling that woman. Get back in line.

Sarah hastily gets back into line

Now then—are you, or are you not, one?

Sarah Pardon?

Port I said . . . are you one?

Sarah No. But I've got an uncle in the Girl Guides I'm not sure about.

Port Oooooooooh. I think we'll forget the numbers. We'll do some mop drill instead. (*Moving* DR) Team, atten-shun.

Everyone stands to attention

Shoulder mops.

Everyone lifts their mops with the right hand and transfers it to their left shoulder. At this point, the mops of Sarah, Alderman, Jack and Starboard shoot over their shoulders and fall. Only Dick and Alice complete the manoeuvre correctly

(*Annoyed*) Pick 'em up. Pick 'em up. Pick 'em up.

There is a scramble for the mops

That was disgraceful. Absolutely disgraceful. (*He snatches Sarah's mop*) Let me show you how it should be done.
Starboard You?
Port Yes, me. For your information, I used to be a Sea Scout.
Sarah Yes. But he had to give it up when his tent sank.

They all laugh

Port Silence. Silence. Now watch this. (*He stands* C, *back to the audience and performs the manoeuvre*) Hup, two three, four. (*Snatching the mop from his shoulder he hurls it to the floor at Sarah's feet*) Like that.
All Oh. Like *that.*

Sarah picks up the mop again

Port (*shouting*) Atten-shun. Shoulder—mops.
All Hup, two, three, four. (*All repeat his actions, then hurl their mops at his feet joyfully*)
Port Pick 'em up. Pick 'em up. Pick 'em up.

They retrieve their mops once more

(*Grimly*) I'm going to give you one more chance. Now get those mops back on your shoulders and we'll do some marching.

They all put their mops on their left shoulder with the exception of Alderman, who puts his on his right

Not *that* shoulder. *This* one. (*He taps his own left shoulder*)

Alderman promptly puts his mop on Port's left shoulder. Port thrusts it back at him and plonks it on to his correct shoulder

(*Moving back* DL) Left turn.

All turn L, *but Sarah, who turns* R

No. No. Turn the other way.

All turn to face the opposite direction

As you were. As you were.

Jack Oooh, I do wish you'd make your mind up.

With much grumbling and jostling they finally all end up facing L, *with their mops on their left shoulders*

Port By the left—quick march.

Everyone but Sarah sets off marching L. *Sarah takes several steps backwards before suddenly surging forward again and following the others*

> *They march in a large circular path, and as they cross centre front the second time, Port steps in front of Alice to lead them round and across the back and off* UR

Sarah, busily smiling and simpering at the audience, fails to notice this and continues in a straight line, crashing into the proscenium arch (or tormentor). She doubles up with anguish, clutching her bosom

Sarah Ooooooh, that's twice this week. And on the same piece of scenery. Talk about making your eyes water.

> *Tommy enters* DR

Tommy (*tugging at her skirt urgently*) Meowww. Meowww.
Sarah (*looking down*) Oh, it's Tommy. And where've you been all morning? Not up in the crow's-nest again?

Tommy nods and puts one paw above his eyes to indicate he's been looking out

Oh, I see. You've been on "look-out"? And have you sighted land?

Tommy shakes his head and indicates upwards urgently

(*Looking up*) Ooooooh. A nasty big storm cloud. And it's heading this way. That's funny. The weather forecast last night said it would be partly sunny, partly windy and partly accurate. Here ... we'd better go warn everybody. Come on.

Sarah hurries off R, *followed by Tommy*

King Rat enters DL *as the Lights begin to dim*

Rat (*triumphantly*)   This time there's no escape for him.
Now comes the hour I crave.
The magic storm I've summoned up
Will send them *all* to watery grave.
(*Loudly*) Come thickening cloud and raging sea,
Come thunder, lightning, rain.
The Pickled Herring sinks today
And I triumph *again*. (*He holds his arms high*)

There is a great crash of thunder and the lights flicker

Fairy Bow-Bells enters DR

Fairy   Once more you're counting chicks un-hatched.
Although by tempest tossed
This gallant ship will founder ...
Still, *not one life* will be lost.

You'll rue the hour you did this deed,
O, creature most abhorrent.
Today you made your last mistake
And signed your *own* death warrant.

Fairy exits

The Lights flicker again

Rat (*laughing*) We'll see, my foolish fairy friend.
Your wings quite soon I'll clip.
But now, farewell to one and all ...
King Rat deserts the sinking ship.

He bellows with laughter and exits

There is another great crash of thunder and Lights flicker madly

Sailors and passengers run about in panic, yelling in fright. Dick staggers on, his arm around Alice. Tommy follows. All are buffeted from side to side as the storm grows worse

Starboard (*in the confusion*) We're sinking. We're sinking.

There are loud yells from the others

Port (*loudly*) Abandon ship. Abandon ship.

The storm continues as the scene ends in confusion

SCENE 4

The shores of Morocco

A deserted beach, flanked with palm trees and rocks. Brilliant sunshine floods the scene

Alderman Fitzwarren enters L looking bedraggled and exhausted

Alderman (*groaning*) I'm the only one saved from the wreck.

He exits R

Dick, Alice and Tommy enter L

Dick Thank goodness we managed to swim to safety.
Alice Yes. But we're the only ones saved from the wreck.

They exit R

Port and Starboard enter L

Port
Starboard } (*together*) We're the only ones saved from the wreck.

They exit R

Jack enters L, wearing nothing but a barrel supported by braces

Jack Oooh, I am fed up.

Audience reaction

I'm the only one saved from the wreck.

Jack exits R

Sarah enters L, *in an old-fashioned bathing costume*

Sarah (*weakly*) And I'm the wreck they've all been saved from.

Alderman, Port, Starboard and Jack all re-enter R. *They greet her*

Alderman Oh, thank goodness everyone's all right. But where are we?
Sarah (*looking around*) Torquay.
Alderman (*puzzled*) Torquay?
Sarah Yes. Everywhere you look, there's palms waving. (*She extends her hand grasping for money*)
Port No, no. It's not Torquay, but it's just as scarey.
Starboard (*worried*) How do you mean? Scarey?
Port Well, look at it. Palm trees, sand and hot sunshine. It's exactly the kind of place you might find *cannibals*.
Sarah (*nervously*) Cannibals?
Jack Hey—he's *right*. My uncle was a missionary and he came to a place just like this to convert cannibals.
Alderman And did he do it?
Jack Course he did. They *loved* him. He gave 'em their first taste of religion.
Starboard Oo-er. I don't think I like it here very much. I want to go home.
Jack Oh, there's nothing to be scared of. If there were any cannibals around here, my mates in the audience would shout and tell us. (*To the audience*) Wouldn't you kids?

Audience reaction

You see?

Alderman Well, Dick and Alice have gone looking for a McDonalds, so while we're waiting for them to come back, why don't we have a little sing-song? It'll help to pass the time.
Port Good idea. What shall we sing?
Jack How about the Income Tax song? *Everything I have is yours.*
Starboard No, no. I don't like that one. Let's do *She's only a surgeon's daughter, but she sure knows how to operate.*
Alderman No, no. Let's sing something we *all* know. How about (*he names a well-known song*)?

All agree

Port What key are we going to sing it in?
Sarah Er—how about a skeleton key?
Jack What's *that*?
Sarah One that'll fit anything.
Jack Right. (*To the audience*) And don't forget ... If you see any cannibals—give us a shout.

Song 11 (Alderman, Sarah, Jack, Port and Starboard)

They begin to sing the song. After a few lines . . .

A dusky figure in a frightening mask, grass skirt and bone necklace appears
L. *He carries a large spear. He moves behind them, in a menacing attitude*

As the audience shouts, the singers fall silent

Sarah What is it? What's the matter?
Jack They're saying there's somebody behind us.
Alderman (*nervously*) Oh, dear. Perhaps we'd better have a look.
Port Good idea.
Starboard F—f—follow me.

To creepy music, they tiptoe L, *and follow round in a circle, the masked figure
tagging along behind. At last they are back in their original positions*

Jack (*to the audience*) There's nobody there at all. You're having us on.

The audience continue shouting

Alderman Oh . . . they say it's the *other* way.
Port Right. We'll look the other way.

They tiptoe round again R, *the figure tagging on and unseen. They arrive back
in their original positions*

Sarah Oh, they're pulling our legs. There's nobody there. Let's go on with
the song.

*All agree, and the song continues. The figure steps forward and taps
Fitzwarren*

Alderman looks round, screams with fright and runs off R, *chased by the
figure*

The others stop singing

Starboard Here—where's Fitzy?
Jack He must be going back to the wreck for his sun-tan lotion. But never
mind. We can go on singing without him.

They begin singing again

*The figure returns and taps Port who turns, reacts and exits in fright chased
by the figure*

The singers fall silent. After ad-lib conversation, they begin again

The figure enters and this time taps Starboard and chases him off

Jack and Sarah re-commence singing

The figure returns, taps Jack and chases him off

Sarah (*calling*) Jack—come back. (*Nervously*) Oo-er. I'm all alone. By
myself and nobody with me. I'll have to sing on my own. (*She begins to
sing in a quavery voice*)

The figure enters and taps her

She turns and looks at it

The figure screams in terror and dashes off

Sarah looks after it in surprise, then turns to the audience and shrugs

Well—you can't win 'em all, can you?

She trudges after the figure

There is a rapid fade to a Black-out for the end of the scene

SCENE 5

The Sultana's palace

The throneroom of a splendid palace in Moorish style, reflecting the great riches of its owner, Sultana Bunn. The Royal Throne is CB *atop a dais, and burly Nubian Slaves (or Handmaidens) stand at each side of it supporting large fans on long poles. Two large dishes, overflowing with diamonds and other precious stones, are situated at the foot of the throne, one to each side. The scene is warmly lit*

When the scene begins, the Sultana is seated on her throne watching dancers in brightly coloured silks and satins performing an exotic Eastern-inspired routine, whilst others dress the room beating time with tambourines and finger cymbals. Zubediah, a favoured slave, sits on the edge of the dais R

Dance (Dancers)

At the end of the dance, the dancers prostrate themselves before the Sultana. She gives them a dismissive wave and they withdraw to mingle with the others as she rises and moves down CF *followed by Zubediah*

Sultana (*sighing*) I don't know where they find the energy. They haven't eaten a decent meal in weeks. (*Sighing again*) Oh, Zubediah—what I wouldn't give to taste a nice juicy apple again. But it's no use. There's not one left in the country. They've all been eaten by those awful rats.
Zubediah Not all, Great Sultana. (*She produces an apple*) I've been saving this for you since Christmas.
Sultana (*delightedly*) Ahhhhh, Zubediah. You shall have your freedom in return for this piece of fruit. Oooh, I can't wait to get my teeth into it.

She reaches out for it but before she can take it . . .

A huge rat runs on, snatches it out of Zubediah's hand and runs off again

Everyone recoils in horror, and the two Nubian slaves leap on to the throne, screeching and stamping their feet in fright

(*Miserably*) It took my apple. (*She begins to cry*)

Zubediah (*quickly*) Don't worry, O Gracious One. I have another. (*She gets out a second apple*) See?

Sultana (*fighting back tears*) Oh, Zubediah. Whatever would I do without you? (*She holds out her hand*)

The room suddenly fills with rats

There is instant panic. The Sultana covers her face with her hands. Zubediah screams and the apple shoots into the air

It is caught by a rat and they all rush off, squealing with excitement

(*Furiously*) Oh, I hate those rats. I hate them, I hate them, I hate them.

Zubediah (*miserably*) If only we knew how to get rid of them. But we've tried everything, and still they torment us. Soon there'll be nothing left to eat in the entire country.

Sultana Let's talk about something else, Zubediah. Tell me about the strangers who were captured this morning.

Zubediah Your wish is my command, Great Sultana. There are seven of them. Four men, two women and a strange-looking creature covered in soft fur.

Sultana (*frowning*) I must see this wonder for myself. Have them brought before me at once.

Zubediah signals L

The prisoners and Tommy enter L

Everyone stares at Tommy and the Court buzzes with amazement. The two Nubians quickly jump down and re-take their original positions

Jack (*glancing around*) So this is the (*local night-spot*).

Sultana Who *are* you? And what brings you to my unfortunate country?

Dick If it please Your Majesty, our ship, *The Pickled Herring*, sank in a great storm and we were cast ashore just a few miles from here. We had to sleep on the beach all night.

Sarah Yes. And it was a very exclusive beach as well. It was so posh, they wouldn't even let the tide in.

Sultana And what manner of beast is that? (*She points at Tommy*)

Dick Why, that's Tommy ... my cat.

Sultana (*puzzled*) Cat?

Alice (*to Tommy*) Say hallo to Her Majesty, Tommy.

Tommy sits up and bows

Sultana (*delighted*) I like this—*cat*. I will have him.

Dick (*quickly*) Oh, I'm afraid Tommy isn't for sale, Your Majesty.

Tommy shakes his head

He's my friend, you see? I couldn't part with him.

Alderman Out of the question.

Sultana But after your heads are chopped off, he will need a *new* friend. And there is plenty of room for him here.

There is a shocked reaction

Port (*dismayed*) After our *whats* are chopped off? (*He clutches his throat*)

Starboard But you can't do *that*, missis. We've grown quite attached to them.

Sultana (*annoyed*) I beg your pardon. I can do what I like. I am Sultana of Morocco.

Sarah I don't care if you're Banana of Bagdad. You're not chopping *my* head off. I wouldn't be able to see where I was going.

Zubediah I'm afraid we have no choice. Morocco is a poor country and we have so little food, it was decreed that all strangers must be put to death so the rest of us would have enough to eat.

Alice But that's ridiculous. How can you possibly claim to be poor? Look at those jewels (*she indicates them*) and the beautiful clothes you're all wearing.

Sultana Jewels. Rich clothing. Yes. We have much more than we could ever need. But when it comes to food—*then* we are poor. No matter what we grow or what we buy, the rats devour it. The entire palace is swarming with them and our storehouses are as empty as our stomachs.

Dick Then maybe we're just the people you're looking for. Tommy's the best rat-catcher in the world. He'll soon get rid of them for you.

The Moroccans look interested

Sultana This—cat. He will chase away the rats?

Dick Once Tommy gets to work, there won't be a rat left for miles. And once they're gone, Alderman Fitzwarren here can supply you with all the food you can eat.

Sultana He can?

Jack (*brightly*) You name it, and Fitzwarren's Store will supply it. Isn't that right, Fitzy?

Alderman Why—er—yes. Yes.

Zubediah (*longingly*) Oh, just think of it, Your Majesty. To be able to *eat* again. (*Dreamily*) Food.

Sultana Food.

Moroccans Food.

The whole Court almost swoons at the thought

Song 12 (Zubediah, Sultana and Company)

Sultana Very well. If this cat can do as you say, Stranger, I will spare your lives and reward you with riches beyond belief. Not only that, we will return you to your own country and purchase everything that Fitzwarren's Store has to offer.

Alderman (*eyes widening*) Oooooh. I'm going international.

Sultana Let the fight begin.

Everyone retreats to create a fight area as ...

Rats suddenly flood the stage

To shouts of encouragement from everyone, Tommy does battle with them. Quickly and efficiently, he kills several with ease. Squealing with fright, the survivors hurry off with Tommy in pursuit. There is much rejoicing and the dead bodies are quickly removed by the Moroccans

(*Delightedly*) Your lives are spared, Strangers. Even now the corridors of my palace are filling with the bodies of our tormenters, and soon they will all be gone.

King Rat suddenly appears L, *sword in hand*

All cower back in surprise

Rat (*snarling*) Not so. For I, King Rat, remain ...
You've made a big mistake.
For ev'ry rat who now lies dead
Revenge I mean to take.
Both Whittington and yonder cat
I'll kill without delay,
As for the rest—your time will come
Before the break of day.
I'll summon rats the whole world wide
And though you vainly strive
To keep them out, I swear
I'll watch them eat you all alive.
(*He steps forward, sword ready*)

Fairy Bow-bells enters with a sword

Fairy Fear not, brave Master Whittington.
This sword will match his any time.
'Tis forged from ancient London Bells:
Its aim? To end *his* life of crime.

Quickly, Dick accepts the proffered sword and faces King Rat. As the two circle warily, all the others retreat to the outer perimeters of the room. King Rat lunges with his sword, but Dick dances back and out of reach. Again Rat strikes out, and Dick once more skips out of reach. Rat thrusts a third time and Dick counters it with his own sword. There is a great clanging of bells and Rat drops his sword, flinging up his hands to cover his ears and wailing in agony. Dick lunges with his sword and stabs him. Rat falls to the floor, dead. Everyone rejoices

So dies "King Rat". A fitting end,
Well worth this rousing cheer.
But England calls for your return.
It's time to leave for home, I fear.
Within the famous Guildhall soon
You'll find your great renown.
Sir Richard Whittington, you'll be:
Four times Lord Mayor of London Town.

Everyone reacts

Rat is carried out by the Nubians

Sultana Then we bid you goodbye, Richard Whittington. But as I promised, you shall not leave empty-handed. One of our largest ships will carry you, laden with gold and diamonds as a small token of our thanks for what you have done for us.

Dick I thank you, Your Majesty. And we'll see it returns filled with the best food Fitzwarren's Store can provide. Even better—why not come to London with us? With Alderman Fitzwarren's permission, I'd like to marry Alice, and you could be Guest of Honour at our wedding.

Sarah And ours.

She simpers at Jack who looks sick

Sultana The idea pleases me. Zubediah shall come too.

Alderman (*beaming*) Then if Alice agrees, so do I.

Alice (*moving to Dick*) With all my heart.

Everyone congratulates them

Fairy   Then back to London without delay
                              Where we'll meet again on their Wedding Day.

Everyone cheers. There is a reprise of the opening song to the show, then the scene ends in general celebration

SCENE 6

Outside the Guildhall

Jack enters

Jack Oooh, I am fed up.

Audience reaction

No. I'm only pulling your leg, this time. I'm not fed up at all. In fact— since we got back to London, I've been having a smashing time what with one thing and another. Here—and you'll never guess what. Old Fitzy's made me manager of the whole shop *and* put my wages up to twenty p a week. Mind you—I'm not thinking about retiring yet. By the time I've paid my National Insurance, my Income Tax, my Pension Scheme and the Poll Tax, I have to give the Government fifty pounds a week out of my savings. Still—money isn't everything, is it? It can't buy you happiness. But if you've plenty, you can at least be miserable in comfort. Anyway— never mind about all that. What I've come out here for, is to tell you that you're all invited to Dick and Alice's wedding. The only thing is . . . they want a big choir to do all the singing and the Huddersfield Choral Society hasn't been formed yet, so we wondered if *you'd* help us out. Will you do that? Will you? Oh—great. Right. Well first of all, we'll have a little practise to see how much noise you can make. I'll sing you a little song so you'll know what we're going to do, and then you can have a go at it and I'll see if you're any good. All right? One song coming up.

Song 13: Song Sheet (Jack)

(*Note: If desired, Port and Starboard can join Jack after the first rendering of the song by the audience. The song sheet can then be worked out between the three of them in competition form*)

At the end of the song, there is a quick fade for the end of the scene

SCENE 7

The Guildhall and Finale

The interior of the great Guildhall, hung with flags and banners. Full lighting

Song 14 (Full Company)

Babes
Juniors
Senior Chorus
Sultana and Zubediah
Fairy and King Rat
Port and Starboard
Alderman Fitzwarren
Jack and Sarah
Tommy
Dick and Alice

Dick Our pantomime is over. Its merry course has run.
Alice We hoped you've all enjoyed our songs, our dancing and our fun.
Jack But now it's time to say "Good-night", and so, we'll do just that.
Sarah Good Luck, Good Health, God Bless, from us—the cast of Whittington.
All And his cat.

There is a reprise of the Finale song then—

the final CURTAIN *falls*

FURNITURE AND PROPERTY LIST

ACT I

SCENE 1

On stage: Timber and plaster houses
Frontage of Fitzwarren's Stores with mullioned windows and practical
  door
Other shops

Off stage: Rolling pin **(Sarah)**
Bundle on stick **(Dick)**
String with tin cans tied to tail **(Tommy)**
Rat **(Tommy)**
Posy of flowers **(Alice)**

Personal: **Fairy:** wand (required throughout)
Dick: purse on belt

SCENE 2

On stage: Nil

No props required

SCENE 3

On stage: Long counter. *On it:* empty children's shoe-boxes. *Under it:* slab of
  mouldy bacon
Safe
Other dressing as required

Off stage: Box wrapped in brown paper marked "Fragile", containing broken glass
  and metal **(Dick)**

During black-out on page 22:

Strike: Box

Set: Besom for **Dick**
Coins, small sac for **Alderman**
Dick's bundle and stick

Personal: **Dick:** purse on belt

SCENE 4

On stage: Nil

Personal: **Jack:** arm sling

SCENE 5

On stage: Grassy knoll
          Milestone indicating "5 miles to London"

Off stage: Bundle on stick, containing small piece of cheese and tiny crust of bread
          (Dick)

Personal: **Dick:** handkerchief

ACT II

SCENE 1

On stage: Bulk of *The Pickled Herring*
          Steps leading up to it
          Ship's Chandlers with practical door
          The Beaux Legs Inn with practical door
          Boxes etc.
          Other dressing as required

Personal: **Sarah:** coin in pocket

SCENE 2

On stage: Nil

No props required

SCENE 3

On stage: Deck of *The Pickled Herring*
          Buckets, long-handled mops
          Deck dressing as required

Off stage: 6 long mops **(Starboard)**

SCENE 4

On stage: Palm trees
          Rocks

Off stage: Barrel and braces **(Jack)**
          Spear, mask, bone necklace **(Dusky figure)**

SCENE 5

On stage: Throne on dais
          2 large dishes overflowing with diamonds and precious stones
          2 large fans (for **Slaves** or **Handmaidens**)
          Tambourines, finger cymbals (for **Dancers**)
          Sword **(Rat)**
          Sword **(Fairy)**

Personal: **Zubediah:** 2 apples

SCENE 6

On stage: Nil

Off stage: Song sheet **(Jack)**

SCENE 7

On stage: Flags, banners

LIGHTING PLOT

Property fittings required: *nil*

Various simple interior and exterior settings

ACT I, Scene 1

To open: Bright, sunny exterior lighting

Cue 1	**Tommy** exits after rat DR *Dim lighting*	(Page 7)
Cue 2	**King Rat** exits *Return to previous lighting*	(Page 8)

ACT I, Scene 2

To open: General exterior lighting

Cue 3	At end of Song 3 *Fade to black-out*	(Page 15)

ACT I, Scene 3

To open: General interior lighting

Cue 4	**Dick:** "... you ordered this morning." Trio react in dismay *Snap black-out; then green follow-spot on* **King Rat**	(Page 20)
Cue 5	**King Rat** exits with a laugh of triumph *Cut follow-spot; bring up light to half*	(Page 21)
Cue 6	**Dick**'s eyes close, **Tommy** stretches *Begin to slowly fade lighting to semi-darkness*	(Page 22)
Cue 7	**King Rat** appears DL *Green follow-spot on him*	(Page 22)
Cue 8	**King Rat** exits *Cut green spot; fade to complete black-out; then increase slowly to full*	(Page 22)
Cue 9	**Sarah** and **Alice** comfort each other *Fade to black-out*	(Page 24)

ACT I, Scene 4

To open: General lighting

Cue 10	At end of Song 6 *Black-out*	(Page 27)

ACT I, Scene 5

To open: General exterior lighting

No cues

ACT II, Scene 1

To open: General exterior lighting

No cues

ACT II, Scene 2

To open: Lighting to indicate shadow of warehouse

Cue 11   With a howl of rage, **Port** chases **Starboard** off L   (Page 38)
           Black-out

ACT II, Scene 3

To open: General exterior lighting

Cue 12   **King Rat** enters DL   (Page 43)
           Begin to dim lights

Cue 13   **Rat:** "And I triumph *again*."   (Page 43)
           Lights flicker

Cue 14   **Fairy** exits   (Page 44)
           Lights flicker

Cue 15   **Rat** bellows with laughter and exits   (Page 44)
           Lights flicker madly—continue till end of scene

ACT II, Scene 4

To open: Brilliant sunshine

Cue 16   **Sarah** trudges after figure   (Page 47)
           Rapid fade to black-out

ACT II, Scene 5

To open: Warm interior lighting

No cues

ACT II, Scene 6

To open: General exterior lighting

Cue 17   At end of Song 13   (Page 52)
           Quick fade to black-out

ACT II, Scene 7

To open: Full general lighting

No cues

EFFECTS PLOT

ACT I

Cue 1   At end of Song 1   (Page 1)
               Flash

Cue 2   As Lights begin to brighten again   (Page 22)
               Handbell, Man's voice as page 22

Cue 3   **Fairy** waves wand and exits   (Page 29)
               Bells (to tune of "Oranges and Lemons")—faint at first, then
               increasing in volume as **Dick** *speaks*

Cue 4   As chorus voices die away   (Page 29)
               Fade bells to ring softly for another stanza

ACT II

Cue 5   **Rat:** "And I triumph *again*."   (Page 43)
               Crash of thunder

Cue 6   **Rat** bellows with laughter and exits   (Page 44)
               Crash of thunder, storm effect—continue till end of scene

Cue 7   **Dick** thrusts at **Rat** with his sword   (Page 50)
               Clanging of bells—fade as everyone rejoices

MADE AND PRINTED IN GREAT BRITAIN BY
LATIMER TREND & COMPANY LTD PLYMOUTH
MADE IN ENGLAND